The Sanctamooja and Me

The Sanctamooja and Me

Melvin Brown

CONTENTS

MY LIFE THE FIRST PART

I WAS BORN in Spokane, Washington, in 1940 to Gail and Virginia Brown, and of course, I was the most beautiful baby they had ever seen. I was named after my uncle Melvin; he died before I was born. My first memory was when I was three years old. My dad was drafted into the army, and I remember going with my dad to the bus stop that was in front of our house; my mom was sitting on the front steps, crying. I wasn't sure why she was crying, and my dad took me to the bus stop with him and told me that he had to go away for a long time and that I would have to take care of my mother while he was gone. I never forgot that. He told me that he loved me as he left on the bus. Anyway, that is the first and one of the most important memories that I have.

My mother was able to join Dad in California while he was in boot camp, so I spent my time with my grandparents. Mom came home, and Dad went to Japan. Mom got sick and went to the hospital. I went to my grandparents' farm to live while Mom got well, and my dad came home from the war. I remember when Dad came home, he took Mom and me to a little restaurant for dinner, and the jukebox kept playing "I'm Looking over a Four-Leaf Clover." I found out later that that was one song people loved because the war was over and everyone was looking over a four-leaf clover to better times.

In 1945, I started my great educational journey. It did not sit too well with me. I started school at Columbia Elementary that was in East Hilliard Heights. I went there until the third grade. We then moved to the Spokane Valley where I attended Trentwood Elementary through the eighth grade. I then went on to my higher education—all four years of it—at West Valley High School. All through my educational career, my parents heard the same story, which was, "Heck of a likeable kid, he just doesn't get it?" Now, I think I got it all right; I was just smart enough to not let them know it. And finally, when I got all the way through school, there was a big sigh of relief from my mom, dad, and me. I could finally get on with the plans I had for my life. But as the saying goes, "The best laid plans of mice and men." So I am going to tell you about the second part of my life. It's a long ride, but it sure has been fun. I would like to take a little time here to tell you some more about my mother. She weighed ninety pounds while soaking wet. She loved her family and took care of us but never babied us. She never said "You wait until your dad gets home." She took care of it herself. But no matter what, we loved her very much. My father was born in Canada because his father had moved from the Washington coast to a homestead in Canada. But due to bad weather, Grandpa Brown then moved his family back to the United States. Dad and his brothers, Gordon and Doran, then grew up in the Arlington-Darrington area on the coast of Washington State. All three brothers went to war; Dad went to Japan, and Gordon and Doran went to Europe. They all came home OK. Dad moved after high school to Spokane and met and married my mom and made the most beautiful baby they had ever seen; that would be me.

Grandpa and his dogs

My dad Gail & Mom Gin

Baby Mel 1940

Gin and Gail
Wedding Day
July 15, 1939

Mom and Dads
Wedding Day
1939

One of his first
dangerous tricks at
nine months old.

Grandma and Grandpa
Brown's Wedding day
17, Aug 1917

My Mom

My Dad WWII

Grandpa and
Grandma Brown

Mom and Uncle
Clarence

MY NAME SAKE MY
UNCLE MELVIN

Bath Time

Grandma and
Grandpa Lewis

Me at age 3

Mom & Me

Dad and me

Mel in Grandma Lewis's Garden

My dad brought this
suit to me when he came
home from the service.

Mels first day of school

Dad and me

Gail and Gin
Fort Roberts, CA.

THE SECOND PART

A S I SAID, I spent a big part of my early life on my grandparents' farm in beautiful northern Idaho. I want to tell you a little about my grandmother. She was a big part of my life. She lived to be ninety-four years old. She married my grandfather when she was fourteen years old, and they were married for forty-eight years. They were married until the death of my grandfather, and they were in love every day of those forty-eight years. She canned on her old wood-burning cookstove. She put up enough food for the whole year, and let me tell you, we ate very well. So now I would like to talk more about northern Idaho and our farm. It is a land of mountains, lakes, and rivers. We had no electricity until 1957. We did everything with the sun or lamp oil. How did we ever survive? We milked cows and raised pigs, horses, rabbits, chickens, dogs, and cats. We also ate deer meat; it was called government mule by everyone we knew. Shoot, I was twenty-one years old before I knew that people hunted deer in the daylight. We hunted elk from horseback right from our own ranch. I grew up on the shores of beautiful Lake Coeur d'Alene. It is so funny to me how everyone today must try to eat fish if they can afford to buy it at the market when all we did was walk down to the lake and catch trout, perch, sunfish, catfish, crappie, and bass. We didn't have super-duper lures or wooly bugger flies. All we used was garden hackle, also known as big old fat worms. Just an old cork float, a hook, and two split-shot sinkers made of lead, which we crimped with our teeth without too much brain damage. Anyway, we caught all the fish we needed. Each bay on the lake had a dock where all the farmers had their mailboxes. Because our mail was delivered by boat, oh, it was so much fun to meet the mail boat every day. Lake Coeur d'Alene is a very big lake. It has about 110 miles of shoreline. It is about forty miles long. It has three rivers running into it. They are the Coeur d'Alene River. It starts close to the Montana border and winds through the northern panhandle and runs into Coeur d'Alene Lake. We fished and floated every square inch of it as kids. It has beautiful westslope cutthroat trout. Then there is the Saint Joe River.

It is over one hundred miles long and is designated as a wild and scenic river. It also is loaded with westslope cutthroat trout. It empties into Lake Coeur d'Alene. Then there is the Saint Maries River. It also empties into the lake through the Saint Joe River. We fished all of these rivers as kids and still do today. So as you can see, I had a well-rounded education. It just didn't all happen in school. So I guess I will start by talking about my childhood adventures, so hang on, and I am sure by the end of this story, you will wonder how I and my brothers are still alive.

Uncle Boyd WWI
1917

Brother Doran
National Guard

Uncle Boyd Harlow
June 1972

Uncle Boyd in front of his 1936 Ford

Uncle Boyd down on the farm

Grandma Lewis in front of farmhouse

Brother Doran Age 7   Doran Age 8

Mel holding baby brother Doran

Winter on the farm. The front peak of the barn is
where Uncle Boyd and I took the wasp nest down.

The barn on a winter day looking down
from the apple orchard.

Beauty Bay, Idaho

Ice on Coeur d'Alene Lake in front of our farm.

Gordy, grandma, Mel & Doran

Mom, dad and Mel with friends.

Mel and little brother Gordon

Mel, Doran and Rod Olund
in front of farm house.

Mel and Doran in sled
grandpa Lewis built for Mel
when he was born. Mom
and Dad didn't have a car so
they pushed me everywhere.

Mel and the famous
outhouse.

See, I'm the
best tree climber
in Northern Idaho

Mel and Rod
playing cowboys

My Dad

Love that bubble gum

Mel and cat
Echo Bay

Mel and dad at
Priest Lake Idaho

Mom, Doran and Mel

Doran and Mel

Grandpa splitting wood

Mel and Sharon

Mel and Dad

Good day of fishing

Doran and Mel thinking
of something to do.

Brother Doran 3
at Echo Bay

Doran and Mel   Mel and Doran at
                                 MT Rainier, WA

Mel and Doran on the   Doran, Mom and me
Pony Lake Express

Mom and Uncle Clarence

My horse Cricket

Cricket and my dog Mishka.

My horses in the hay field.

My first woodshop

It's not easy getting
icicles from the house

Doran, Mel and Dad

Fishing off the dock
at Echo Bay.

Spring time at Echo Bay

Brothers Gordy &
Doran on the farm

On the farm with
Grandpa and Grandma

Mel and friend Rod
in Dog Town

Mel with fish
he caught.

CHRISTMAS STORIES

CHRISTMAS 1944, I was four years old, and my dad was still overseas, so Mom and I were staying with my grandparents. Christmas eve—it's time for me to hang up my sock. Well, I was just getting ready to hang it on the mantel when Grandpa came in. He had a giant sock and a big metal washtub. I asked him what he was doing. And this was what he told me: "I'm going to hang this big old sock up." He hung his sock up, then he put the washtub under the sock. He showed me that there was a hole in the toe of the sock and it had a tennis ball in the hole. He then told me that when Santa came that night, he would start putting good stuff in his big old sock, and the tennis ball would fall out. Santa would keep stuffing his sock, and the presents would fall into the washtub, and he would get way more stuff than I would in my little old sock. Well, I was only four years old, but I knew this wasn't right. I went running to Grandma and told her that Grandpa was going to cheat Santa. Grandma said, "Don't worry because I know that Santa is much smarter than your grandpa is." So I went off to bed, but I was not happy. Well, Christmas morning came. I ran downstairs and saw that my grandpa had a sour look on his face. I saw my sock had all kinds of good stuff in it. I looked at Grandpa's sock, and the washtub was full. It had an old rubber boot with a big hole in it, a big half-rotten squash, some chunks of coal, an old broken shovel, etc. I guess Grandma was right after all; Santa is smarter than Grandpa.

Christmas 1945, I was five years old. Dad was not home yet but soon would be, and we were still staying with my grandparents.

A little history about my father—he was in Japan in the Second World War. His two brothers were in the European theater. All three came home OK. I thank God for that and for all the men that have gone before. Thank you, and may God bless you always.

We were trimming the Christmas tree. Grandpa came in, and he had all of these walnuts that he had painted silver and put a yarn loop on to hang them with. Well, I think they're neat, but that's about it. Christmas morning, I came down, and I started opening my presents. Grandpa said, "Why don't you open one of those walnuts?" I said, "Naw, I got to open my presents." I threw wrapping paper and ribbon this way and that. Well, Grandpa kept after me. Finally, I said, "OK." So I cracked a walnut open, and a penny fell out. Now I was opening walnuts; There were dimes, nickels, and pennies. When I got done, I had about a dollar fifty, and that's big money in 1945. But what I think of this is that my grandfather thought enough of me to take the time to cut the walnuts open, take the meat out for Grandma to cook with, then put a coin in and glue each one back together just to make a little five-year-old boy happy on Christmas morning. Sixty-five years later, I don't remember anything else I got that Christmas, but I remember the walnuts and the love that went into making them. That might be something for young parents to think about as they read this; it really is the little things that count the most.

One more grandpa story. As I have said before, we would walk down to the general store, and we would be walking, and he would stop and sniff the air, and he would say, "I think that over behind that stump there is a Nehi Root Beer bottle." I would run over there, and he was right. By the time we would get to the store, I would have ten- or fifteen-cents worth of bottles. But again, I just wonder how he took the time to hide those bottles and then remember where they were, all hidden just for me. As you can tell by now, my grandfather was a very big part of my young life.

My grandfather would take me out with him to cut firewood. I would stack brush, and when I had a big-enough pile, he would start it burning. Then he and I would look around and find two forked willow sticks about three feet long. Then he would pull out a package of saltine crackers. He would give me a cracker and show me how to lay it flat over the fork in the stick, and he would say, "Steady now. Hold it over the fire." We would happily roast our crackers until they were black—best darn crackers I ever did eat. Like I said, it's the little things; thanks, Grandpa.

Well, we now jump ahead to about seven years old. The year 1947, my brother Doran was born. So now, the pressure on me to perform was getting intense. Up to this point, I had things pretty much going my way until this cute little kid came along. But I can say that I love him very much, and we went on to have some great adventures together. But I had to get my game on at that point, so thinking about this brings back a memory. My mom and dad had friends that I know some of you will remember—Bill McCarnis and Bud Thorsen. Anyway, they used to go out to Deer Lake and go fishing, so we're all out there, having a good time. Bill was sitting at a picnic table, and I was on top of the table, so for some reason, I jumped off and did a belly flop. Dang! That hurt, but Bill was laughing his head off. Not wanting to waste a chance to have someone laugh at me, up on the table I went, and you guessed it—another belly flop. Bill was still laughing, so up I went again. Finally, my mother yelled over, "Damn it, Bill, quit laughing at him, or he's going to kill himself." So I guess Mom saved my life, but I think I would have stopped just before passing out.

Speaking of my little brother, I would wrestle with him. Of course, I let him win, but it was the way he won that was hard to take. He always had a wet diaper, so when I was down on my back, he would sit on my head, and then I would make a big show of it, which, I might add, I was good at. Then I would give up. Oh, Mom and Dad thought that was so funny, so I guess it was worth it?

So we move ahead. We had so much fun; we played till after dark in the summer. Hide and seek, kick the can—that's how we split Doran's lip open; we had a bad can. It happens. But cat killer was our best game. I thought it up. I would dress in black clothes, and everyone would look for me. I would do neat things like jump off the garage or a telephone pole or a tree and kill everyone before they could catch me. Sometimes, as I jumped off the garage roof, I thought I might be the one killed. Oh, it was great fun. When we were done, we all had a big drink from that old rubber garden hose. It always had such a distinct taste. I found out much later in life that it might have killed us. Bummer. I remember Mom's friend came up from LA one time. She was so paranoid from living down there that she didn't want her kids playing after dark with us. She asked my mother if she wasn't afraid that someone would kidnap us. Here is what our dear mother told her: "No, because they would bring them back in two hours or less." I think she was right. But I think they would have paid her to take us back. Sure glad she didn't think of that, or we would have been busy.

We played cowboys and Indians. I remember we were playing with Jake. He was the cowboy because he *always* wanted to be the cowboy. So Doran and I were, you guessed it, the Indians. So anyway, we made our raid and caught Jake. We took him out behind his house and tied him to a tree. What we didn't know was there was a yellow jacket nest at the base of the tree. Just as we finished tying him up, here came the yellow jackets, so we *left*. When Jake's mom heard him screaming, she ran out and got him untied. Neither one of them looked too good. But when Dad got done with us, you would have thought our butts were in that yellow jackets nest. One good thing though: Jake never wanted to be the cowboy anymore.

My wise old uncle Boyd never got stung by bees. I asked him why not. He told me that "if you hold your breath, it closes your pores, and they can't sting you." Cool. So Doran and I tried it. We were slapping those suckers and not getting stung. So of course we told Jake about it. Well, he just happened to have a wasp nest on his front porch, so he held his breath, and here came a big wasp. *Clap!* He missed, let his breath out, and got stung right between the eyes—a terrible sight. It got to where Jake didn't want to play with us much. He stayed in the house a lot. We blamed his mom, but I think it might have been his own idea.

I was mowing our lawn one day with our push mower because Dad said it built character. I thought a power mower would build the same amount of character, but Dad wouldn't hear of it. So anyway, I was pushing that sucker. Jake came and wanted me to play, so I told him, "I can't until I get the lawn done." So Jack said he would get his mower and help me. We were going along just fine—him out in front and me right behind. Well, he made a sharp turn, stepped in front of my mower, and *whack*, I cut the tendon in his heel. Doran and I dragged him in to the house. We kind of wanted to stop the bleeding before we sent him home. Mom and Dad came home and followed the blood trail into the house. Mom used to call our place bloody acres. Well, after Jake got out of his cast, we just didn't see much of him. It's like he was hiding from us. That's too bad; look how much fun he was missing out.

THE SANCTAMOOJA AND ME

DO YOU REMEMBER back when I told you that we got our mail by boat on beautiful Lake Coeur d'Alene? Well, every day, just about dusk, we would walk down to the lake to get our mail. Our lane was one quarter of a mile long down to the main road. Then we would cross the main road and then another lane, also one quarter of a mile long, down to the dock to get our mail.

I was seven years old at this time and about as brave as they come. I had to stop and look at everything as Grandpa and I made our way down the lane. I would see the cows and horses in the meadow and also those government mules that I told you about. I loved to mess around the drainage ditch along the lane. I could find garter snakes, frogs, and water skippers. Oh, life was great. So we would get down to the main road, but before we crossed the road, Grandpa would make me stop, look both ways, and wait to see if we could hear anything coming, which we never did. Because you only got a car or truck about once every two hours and that was on a busy day.

But now that I think about it, I remember one morning when Grandpa and I had just turned the cows into the meadow when we heard a truck coming down the gravel road. We watched as a black bear walked out in front of the truck. Old Ben Olsen was driving his international pickup. Well, Ben swerved to miss the bear. He went off the road and tipped up on the driver's side. Grandpa got his old Gibson tractor and hooked on to Ben's truck and pulled it back onto its wheels and back onto the road. I remember old Ben saying, "If I had hit that bear, we could all have had some good eating. Well, see you. I got to get to town."

I told this story about old Ben because I wanted to show you that this took two hours, and in that time, no cars came by. No wrecker or police or police reports to fill out, just two good old boys helping each other out. *Ah,* those were the days.

So as I was saying, it's just before dark, and Grandpa and I were going down to the lake to get the mail, which came by boat every day. All the farms up the draw from our farm had mailboxes on the dock. So as we were walking along, Grandpa was a little bit behind me, and all of a sudden, I heard a big splash in the lake. I jumped and said, "What was that?" Grandpa said, "Whoa, that was a Sanctamooja." I said, "What's a Sanctamooja?" Grandpa said to me, "They live in the lake, but they come out after dark, and they like to go after little boys." I said, "They won't get me. I am the best tree climber in northern Idaho." Grandpa said, "Won't work because Sanctamoojas are the best tree climbers in all Idaho."

"Well, what should I do then?"

Grandpa said, "Just make sure that you don't come down to the lake in the dark—only when I am with you because they don't like big people."

I think that Grandpa was just funning me, but for the last sixty-five years, I have been looking over my shoulder in the dark, looking for a Sanctamooja. I thought I saw one once, but it turned out to be an old garbage bag flapping around in a tree. But I think they are out there because Grandpa said they were.

MOM, THE AVON LADY, AND ME

MOM'S COOKING IN the kitchen, and I was just hanging out when our doorbell rang. I went to open the door, and there stood the Avon lady. Mom told her to come on in. We all went into the front room and sat on the couch. The Avon lady was sitting between Mom and me. The Avon lady was talking to Mom, and they were acting like I didn't even exist. Now, I couldn't have that, so I started to make some of my cute little noises that everyone likes so much. Mom did not seem to be enjoying them at the time, so she told me to knock it off. Well, I figured that she was not going to do anything with the Avon lady there—*wrong*. You see, this was long before a poor, helpless kid could turn his parents in to child protection services. Anyway, I saw the look in Mom's eyes, and I was out the door. Mom went over the Avon lady's lap and out the door right behind me. She caught me about a half block from home. Well, she had a wooden spoon that she had been cooking with, so she got me by the arm and spanked my butt all the way home. We came in the door, and Jazam, the Avon lady was gone. We sat there, wondering why she left. We thought that was kind of a tacky way to treat your customers.

I think Mom was still upset with me for leaving home at such a young age. I was only six years old when I told Mom that I didn't like it there anymore and I was leaving home. I waited for the sobs to start, but Mom just said OK. She went and got out a suitcase and packed my clothes and put me out on the porch. She told me to write now and then so she would know where I was and how I was doing. She said that she hoped I found a good job and a place to live soon as it was cold out. She shut the door, and I heard the *lock* click. I thought that was kind of cold. I thought I wouldn't be calling anytime soon. I did not like that job thing Mom mentioned, and dang, it was kind of cold out. I left, and I dragged that suitcase about half a block before I stopped and thought I could not break my mother's heart like that, so I went back home. I rang the doorbell quite a few times, but Mom must not have heard it because I had to beat on the door to get her attention. She let me back in, but I did not see any tears. She held them in really well. She faked like she was smiling. She was a tough one; maybe that's why I always loved her so much.

IT JUST FELL OFF MY HAND

ANOTHER MEMORY THAT comes to mind: my mom and dad and I were up at Franklin Park one hot August day. I was six years old and just back from leaving home. I think my mom and dad were so glad to have me back home that they were working really hard to make me happy just to make sure that I stayed home this time. *Cool.* Like I said, we were up at Franklin Park. This was back when families actually did things together. Anyway, we spent all afternoon swimming in the pool. Well, I did; Mom and Dad just sat on their blanket, looking at each other. I thought that was a waste of time because there was swimming to be done.

Well anyway, it was time to go home. I changed into my clothes. Mom took my swimsuit. I pumped my chest up and said that I wanted to carry my own swimsuit, and Mom said, "No because you will lose it before we get to the car." Now, do you believe that I was six years old? I just came home for Mom's sake, and she thought I was too young to carry my own swimsuit. But to Mom's credit, she saw the determined look in my eyes and the fact that my dad proudly said, "Ah, let my boy carry his own swimsuit." So she did.

Off we went, walking through the park. Anyway, we got to the car, and Mom said, "Where's your swimsuit?" I looked down at my empty hand and then up into my mother's eyes, and then I said, "I don't know. It just fell off my hand."

ROD AND THE BIG FLIP

ANOTHER TIME, I was about eight years old and one of the best tree climbers around. Tarzan had nothing on me; maybe his monkey did but not Tarzan. Well, there was this big old table in the yard and a big cherry tree with a big limb about eight feet high and about eight feet from the table. I could jump from the table to the limb and swing to the main trunk and slide down to the ground. Well, my friend Rod was scared to try this great feat. Being the great teacher that I was, I took him by the hand and showed him how to flex his knees just right and to spring upward. There was one problem: he flexed his knees and sprang upward all right, but I forgot that his hands were not big enough to hold on to the limb. He just did a big flip and landed on his side and broke his arm in two places.

Now, I was pretty sure that this would be viewed as my fault, so Rod and I decided that falling off the table sounded a lot better.

BEACON HILL SLED RIDE

WE HAD A hill that had a beacon on it because it sat on the hill above the Felts Field Airport that was on the other side of the Spokane River. We kids climbed all over this rocky hill. There was a road that ran up the hill from Dog Town past the water reservoir and on past the beacon. Now in the wintertime, it was our sleigh-riding hill. It was steep and fast. There was not much traffic because no one wanted to drive up or down that hill. You see, as you came past the reservoir, the road made a big turn to the right. After that turn, the road dropped steeply, and at the bottom, there was a greenhouse and a very sharp turn to the left. But if you made the left turn and missed the greenhouse, then it was a straight run until you came to a stop. Now, we always started our run just past the reservoir because it got much steeper after the starting point. Well, one day, I got to thinking, what with me being the best sled rider in northern Idaho and all Eastern Washington, that maybe we ought to start higher on the hill. The guys did not share my enthusiasm for this idea. So I did what I did best: I motivated them to the point that they were too proud to say no. So up we went, clear to the top of the hill. We looked down, and dang, we had never noticed how far down it was to the bottom of the hill before. But none of us were going to chicken out now, on the count of three, we were off. Peat got out first, and then Tom followed, and then I and Rod came behind. I saw Peat hugging the inside of the reservoir corner; he was doing fine until he hit that frozen chunk of ice. He went up the bank and hit the fence that surrounded the reservoir. Tom made the corner OK and headed for the bottom of the hill. Tom got to the greenhouse corner, and he had too much speed going in, so he bailed off his sled, hit the berm, and went straight in the air and through a window in the greenhouse. Tom ended up wrapped around the fire hydrant, but there was enough soft snow that he was OK. I swerved to miss Tom and went across the road and into Mr. Jordan's yard and into his big old Lilac bush, but I was OK. I ran over to see how Tom was doing. He was sitting up and thought he was OK. Then Peat came down, pulling his sled. It had a broken runner, and he said, "I am sure glad that fence was over there, or I would have been swimming." We started laughing about what a great run that was, but all of a sudden, we realized that Rod was not among us. Up the hill we went, looking for him. We heard him crying, and we saw where his sled left the road and went down a steep bank. We found him in some trees; his sled was broken, and yep, you guessed it, Rod had broken his arm again. But you know, we had a great story to tell, and as far as we were concerned, we all made it to the bottom of Beacon Hill from the top.

GETTING RICH

HERE I WAS, eight years old and worrying about my financial future. I had to find out how to get rich. After all, I was eight years old, and time was flying by. All of a sudden, a great opportunity came by. My friend Rod Oland and I were outside my uncle Donks body-and-fender shop. You ask why my uncle is named Donk. Well, of course, his real name is Clarence. But as the story goes, when he was a little boy, he was so stubborn that his buddies started calling him Donkey, which, over the years, got shortened to Donk. Uncle Donks body-and-fender shop was located in Dog town. Well, actually its official name is East Hilliard Heights. But being on the wrong side of the tracks, everyone calls it Dog town, and we and the dogs loved it that way. So we hung out there a lot, learning how to cuss. We just listened and learned. We didn't know what most of it meant, but it sounded good at the time until my mother heard me. One night, I was drying the dishes for Mom when I dropped a dish. I said, "I dropped that damn dish." That's when I found out it was not as cool as I thought it was. And I still can't stand the taste of Ivory soap. Well, as I said, we were looking in the shop doors when my uncle saw us and said hi, so we started talking to him. I told him that we needed to make our fortune. He said, "I have got just the thing for you guys. I just heard that Mr. Keystone is paying for farts." I said, "No way." Uncle Donk said, "Yep, all you have to do is fill up a big old paper bag with farts, and he pays ten cents per fart." So right away, Rod and I could see our fortunes forming right before our eyes. We ran home and found a can of pork and beans and a big old paper bag; we ate the beans and waited. Now, you might think that this was an easy thing to do. Not so. The first one was, but when you get to the second one, you have to have just the right positions so that you don't lose the first one. When you open the bag, you have to be quick and accurate. We lost a few before we got the hang of it. They are lighter than air, you know. Well, this took us half a day to get all twenty farts into that bag. Anyhow, we got it tied off and walked to town. Now, the town of Hilliard was one main street that had some really neat stores, such as the Buffalo Market, which is where Rod and I did most of our heavy-duty shopping—you know, bubble gum, licorice, Sugar Daddies. It had the Chinese Gardens, Keystone's Hardware, Railroad Bar, and Joe's army and navy surplus, which is where we outfitted our outdoor adventures; it was probably the best store in town. So as we went up town, we had to hang on to that bag for fear that it would float away if we let go of it. We went down the main street to Keystone's hardware store. We went in and walked up to Mr. Keystone and said, "Here they are." Mr. Keystone said, "There what is?" We said, "Our bag of farts. Uncle Donk said that you were paying ten cents a fart." Mr. Keystone looked surprised, but he took the bag and asked how many farts we had in the bag. We told him twenty. So he went to the cash register and took out two one-dollar bills and gave them to us. As we left the store, I could see by the look on Mr. Keystone's face that we had made him very happy. As we went out the door, I think he was laughing hysterically. I would think that when he met my uncle at the bar that night that he thanked him for sending us to him to do business because my uncle told us the next day that Mr. Keystone told him we were so good that he had all the farts he needed for a long time to come. Dang, I thought we could do a lot of business with Mr. Keystone. Well, you might say that was the start of my entrepreneurial career. I learned to act fast when an opportunity comes along because who would ever think that you could make 100 percent profit selling farts?

1948

EIGHT YEARS OLD, I am going to tell you what I saw, believe it or not. My mother and I were walking up the lane. Well, actually we were going up the path to the outhouse.

We both heard a noise and looked up. We both saw eight disks on edge, four in front and four behind, and just like that, they were gone. Now, I don't know what they were. I only know what my mom and I saw. It was 1948, and that was the time when people were seeing things in the sky in our area. I thought that it was worth telling at this time. So for what it's worth, it makes me feel better because some people think that I'm nuts. But my mom was there, so that proves it's true.

THE DANCE

YOU KNOW, AS I think back about my eighth year, it is a wonder that I made it to nine. I remember I was at my grandparents' place, and Rod and I were out back, sitting on the roof of the metal shed, just hanging out when along came Carmelita who lived across the street, and she said, "What-cha doing, boys?" Well, that's like putting a red flag in front of a bull. Right away, I jumped up and started dancing around, and of course, I tripped and slid down the roof and right into a pile of junk. I cut my finger pretty bad, and I still have the U-shaped scar on my finger today. Well, I was bleeding but did not want to start crying in front of Carmelita, who by the way thought that this was the funniest thing she had ever seen. So that's when I found out that if you do really stupid things around girls, they really like you. Cool.

I am going to go back a bit because I remember my first week of the first grade. We were in the lunch room, which had no lunch unless you brought your own. This was way before Head Start. So everyone's mom or dad made the kid's lunch, and the kid had to carry it to school. So I got my lunch sack, and just as I opened it, the teacher said, "Melvin, I think you have my lunch." And I said, "Nope, that's the lunch my mom made for me." He said, "Does your mother always make you two big tuna fish sandwiches like that?" So I said, "Yep, when you're a big boy like me, you have to have big tuna fish sandwiches." So the teacher said, "OK." I ate those big sandwiches and got home that night and puked my guts out. I never ate tuna fish sandwiches again until I was halfway through high school.

FISHING

WE HAD A creek that ran through our farm, and we had so much fun playing for hours with our homemade boats or a stick that looked like a homemade boat. Well, this creek ran all the way down to a big beaver pond and over the beaver dam and into the lake. In the spring, rainbow trout would come up the creek and lay their eggs. Then they would hatch, and there were baby fish everywhere. Now, there was a big spring-fed pond in front of the farmhouse. So we kids would go in the late summer as the creek would almost stop running, but it would leave pools of water that trapped the small fish in the pools. So we would get tin cans and go down to catch fish and put them in our tin cans. Now, you watch these modern fishing shows, and they tell you to not touch the fish before you throw them back. Ha! I am here to tell you that we would catch those little fish by our hands and put them in the tin cans and pack them up and put them in Grandpa's fish pond, and they would grow into big fish. We would feed them bread and worms. We enjoyed watching them. They were just like the other pets we kept.

Echo Bay farm, Mel in the creek

Mom by the creek
on the farm.

Front of our farm house.
The fish pond is almost
covered over with snow.

KEYSTONE KOPS

N OW, I WAS about nine years old. At Christmas time, my uncle Clarence thought that it was time for me to have an X-ACTO knife set. Christmas night, I was carving on a model airplane. I was carving toward me when I slipped, and I cut my artery and tendons in my left wrist. I ran into the kitchen where Mom and Dad were. I said, "I cut myself," which they could tell right away because blood was shooting all the way across the room. Dad grabbed me and put me on the couch and made a tourniquet with his belt. Mom called the state patrol, and it so happened that we had a state trooper living up the street. He was working in his garage and had the radio in his patrol car on. He heard the call. He told them that he would get me to the hospital. So off we went—Dad and me in the front seat, Mom in the backseat. We got to the hospital. Dad and I and the cop jumped out and ran into the ER. Mom couldn't get out because there were no door handles on the back doors. This is why my life has been like the Keystone Kops from day one. So as I tell the last part of this adventure, just picture an old Keystone Kop movie. Dad saw that Mom was not there, so he ran out the door, motioned for Mom to come on, and back in the door he went. Mom still couldn't get out. She beat on the windows because there were two guys sitting on a bench, but they weren't about to let a criminal out of a police car. Once again, Dad came to the door, motioned for Mom to come on, and back in he went. Mom was still in the car. Once again, Dad at the door, two guys still sitting there. Finally, Dad figured out why Mom couldn't get out. So he went over and opened the door. Mom jumped out, and a bloody towel fell out, and the two guys were gone, and Mom ran in the door with Dad. And I lived through another adventure. Now, that's funny right there.

Back to my little brother; we slept in the same room, but Doran wanted to sleep with me. Mom would put him in his bed and turn out the light. In the morning, they would find him under my bed. He was too small to climb up on my bed, so he just got under it and went to sleep. Finally, they just threw him in with me, and all was well. But it doesn't end there. We were in school—I in the eighth grade, Doran in the first grade. Because they kicked him out of kindergarten for holding on to a kid's feet while he was on the monkey bars until he fell off, they asked him why he did it. He said, "Because he wouldn't leave my girlfriend alone." So that's why he was a year behind. Anyway, just like the bed thing, he wanted to be with me. So every time the teacher looked the other way, Doran was gone, down to my room, but I had a great teacher; she would hide Doran till his teacher went by, looking for him, and then she would sneak him back down to his room. They finally got him to stay in his room, but he didn't like it much.

MELVIN BROWN

THE HAWK

I HAD AN old wizard motorbike. What's a wizard motorbike you ask? Well, it was a regular bike that had a motor mounted in the frame and a big old pulley mounted on the back rim with a belt drive. It was cool in its day. Anyway, I was driving, and Doran was on the handlebars. Down the road we went, about thirty miles per hour. We saw this big hawk flying over the lake, which is about eight hundred feet below the road. We're watching this hawk, and all of a sudden, I saw Doran's mouth working, but nothing was comeing out. Finally, I followed his eyes and saw that we were within one foot of the edge of the road. Well, I got us back on the road. I did not think Dad needed to know about my great driving skill. So we just went home and cleaned our pants.

LEARNING TO DRIVE

I REMEMBER ONE day when I was about nine years old, Dad and I were in the car, and Dad asked if I wanted to drive. Well, you know the answer to that was heck yes. So Dad drove out to Bigelow Gulch, which is a country road that ran east from Dog town. Well anyway, Dad stopped the car and told me to slide onto his lap. I did, and we started moving. Dad was working the clutch and brakes and gas. Down the road we went, and Dad said, "You steer, OK?" Man, that car steered hard. I could barely see over the hood. I would see a corner coming, and I would start steering with all my might. I found out this driving was a lot harder than I thought. We were driving a 1938 Plymouth, and of course, it had power steering by Armstrong. For all you young guys, this was a great joke in our time, get it? Power steering by Armstrong. So I was steering and about worn out when Dad took over, and my first driving lesson was over. Years later, I figured it all out. While I was steering, my dad had his hand on the bottom of the steering wheel to keep me from steering us off the road. I love my dad a great deal more than I think I ever let him know. I hope someday I get the chance to tell him how much.

As I think about our old cars and all the things they make us do in our cars for safety's sake today, I wonder how we ever made it. A good friend of mine told me something that brought back a memory about seat belts. When we were little guys, we would stand up in the front seat; the only seat belt we had was our dad's right arm. He would put on the brakes and shoot his right arm out and hold you in the seat all at the same time. If he missed a time or two and you kissed the dashboard, you learned to hold on to the back of the seat real tight. How about car seats? We didn't need them. We just stood up behind the front seat and looked out the front window and said, "Are we there yet?" For air conditioning, we just rolled down all the windows. There was nothing like riding around on a hot summer evening with all the windows down. You could smell newly mowed grass. Aw, it was great. You could smell barbeque smoke. This was long before gas barbeques. They actually burned charcoal. All of those fumes would go into your meat. Now that was a burger. I can remember Dad saying, "We're barbequing tonight." I thought I had better have a peanut butter sandwich because Dad would start the barbeque about five o'clock, and about seven o'clock, it might be hot enough to cook on. But like I said, those were the best burgers I ever had. You could smell the sweet summer rain hours before it actually rained. We didn't go anywhere in particular. We just drove around with the car windows down, and at eighteen cents a gallon for gas, it was a great, cheap way for a family to cool off on a hot summer evening, those were the days. Then drive-in movies came along, which were something else for the family to do in their cars. Dad would get us all into the car, and we would get to the drive-in just before dark. We would go on dollar night. Can you believe getting into a movie for a dollar? And we got to see two full-length movies, a news reel, a cartoon, and a coming attraction all for a buck. Hey, that reminds me of the time my brother Doran and a couple of our friends walked to the drive-in movie about two miles from our house. You got in for twenty-five cents if you were walking in. Now, Dad told us, "You watch the first movie and come home." Well, the first movie was so good that we stayed for the second one and then watched the first one again. And just like that, it's midnight. We started walking home. Well, we're about halfway home, and we saw car lights coming, so we jumped off the road and hid because we sure didn't want to be kidnapped. So after the car went by, we started walking home again. Now, there was a car coming the other way, so back in the bushes we went. Well, with all the cars going by and us jumping in the bushes, it took us a long time to get home. When we got there, Dad was gone. But he drove in just after we got home. He said, "You boys are late." I said, "We would have been home sooner, but cars kept coming past, so we had to hide. We did not want to be kidnapped, you know." Dad looked at us and said, "It might have been better if you had been kidnapped." After our butts quit stinging, Dad explained that he was the one in the car, looking for us, and the fact that he had to go to work in about three hours was not sitting too well with him. He explained that we would not be going to the drive-in movies any time soon. But you know, we still got to ride around with the windows all down and smell the sweet smells of summer. And besides that, I knew that dollar night would come around, and there would be a movie that Mom and Dad would have to see. They would not want to leave us home alone, would they?

THE RADIO

I REMEMBER WHEN the radio was king. It was the only thing to listen to. This brings back some great memories. I think that people born after TV need to hear about the old radio stuff. One fond memory I have is on the ranch. Before electricity, Grandpa had a big old battery-powered radio. So it only got used for special programs because you had to save the batteries. I know it's hard to believe that you just couldn't plug the batteries onto a charger. Because guess what? There was no such thing as a battery charger. So as I was saying, Saturday was radio night. I remember sitting there, listening to *Amos and Andy* and *Fibber McGee and Molly*, then of course, there was *Burns and Allen* and oh yeah, don't forget *The Life of Riley*, whose famous saying was "What a revolting development this is." But the best of all was the *Grand Ole Opry* with Roy Acuff, Minnie Pearl, Kitty Wells, the very first queen of country music, and all the other great ones. Now, as I said, Grandpa had this big old radio, and all these programs came out of Spokane, Washington, sixty miles and two mountain ranges from us. I remember this so clearly. I don't know if you will believe this, but it is true. The only way we could get good reception was when Grandpa would sit in his big easy chair with his shoes off; he had a small copper wire hooked up to the radio and wrapped around his big toe. This brought the radio in loud and clear. We would sit in the glow of the oil lamp and listen to the radio. As I have said before, those were the days, and I would not trade those memories for anything.

Grandma Lewis sitting in grandpa's chair.
He always sat here to tune the radio in.

THE FIRE

JAKE AND I were out in the field behind his house. It's late August and about ninety degrees out. The cheat grass was dry, and there was about one acre of it. So out came Jake, and he had a box of wooden matches, and he lit one and blew it out. He got another one out, and I said, "I don't think that is such a good idea." Now, I am not one to tell a guy not to do what he feels is right, but I wasn't too sure about this one. Anyway, Jake lit another match, and for some reason, he dropped it. *Whoosh*, the field was on fire, so I thought it was time for me to go home, and I did.

Well, every man around ran out to fight the fire, and when they finally got the fire out, Jake's dad asked who started the fire, and Jake said, "I cannot tell a lie. Mel did it."

Dad came home, and out behind the house we went. Now, I can honestly say that I earned every spanking I got except this one that I was about to get. All of a sudden, here came Jake's dad, and he had Jake by the ear. "Jake, you tell Mr. Brown who started the fire." Jake was blubbering and said he started the fire and that I had tried to talk him out of it and that he was sorry. But I think he was sorry because he was about to get his butt whipped.

My dad felt so bad because he almost spanked me for something that wasn't my fault. But I thought that I had gotten by with enough stuff without getting caught that I owed him one. But I got out of it OK, so I won after all.

LEAKING BOAT

G RANDPA AND I would walk down to the general store with our fishing poles in the summer. Now, I am always talking about walking three miles to the store. You would think that Grandpa did not have a car; this is not true. He had a beautiful 1937 Chevrolet four-door sedan with suicide rear doors, which almost did my mother in one time. How, you ask? Well, we were going down the road when my mother noticed that her coat was caught in the door, so without thinking, she opened the door. Now, the reason they called them suicide doors is because the door is hinged at the back of the door and they open in the front. So if you open the door when the car is moving, the wind catches the door and pulls it open. Well, my mother was pregnant with my brother Doran at the time, and as she opened the door, it started to pull her out, but my dad grabbed her just in time and kept her from falling out onto the road.

Grandpa thought, with gas at fifteen cents a gallon, why drive just to go three miles to the store? So we walked and had a great time. Well, as I said, we would borrow one of old Bill's wooden rowboats and go fishing. We would get back from fishing, and Grandpa would say, "Dang it, Bill, that boat leaks." Old Bill would say, "That boat doesn't leak." Then Grandpa would say, "Bill, that boat does leak." Then old Bill would say, "If the boat leaked, the water would run out of it." Now, that right there made sense to me.

BUCK

I WANT TO talk to you about a horse that was one of many that I owned over the years. Like I said, we hunted elk from our farm on horseback. We used our horses and mules to pack into wilderness areas to fish and hunt. I have been kicked, bit, bucked off, stepped on, and left behind, but I love those horses. I want to tell you about my favorite horse. His name was Buck, and he was appropriately named. He was eighteen hands high. He was a strawberry roan half-Arabian and half-Tennessee walker. He got his strength from the Arabian half and his ability to walk all day long from his Tennessee walker side. But back to his name; every day when you got on him for the first time, you guessed it, he *bucked*. If you could stay with him until he quit bucking, then you got to ride him all day, and he would go anywhere you wanted and be strong all day. I decided to ride Buck to the top of Coeur d'Alene Mountain and stay overnight. It is seven miles from home, so I took my sleeping bag, and off we went. We got up to the top of the mountain just before dark and I got Buck tied up, and I hiked up to the fire lookout tower, which was not manned that time of year. This was why I only brought my sleeping bag because I knew I could sleep in the tower. Just a little history note: the fire tower is no longer there because they use airplanes to watch for fire now. Well, when I woke up the next morning, I went down to get Buck, and dang, he was gone. He was a master escape artist. He didn't like ropes or fences, and he was good at getting out of both of them. So there I was, seven miles from home with no horse. I tied my sleeping bag onto my saddle and picked it up and started for home. I got to thinking later, *Why don't I just hide my saddle and come back for it later?* No, I carried it all the way home. Doing this really helped my disposition. I was thinking to myself, *when I get home, I am going to lay a two-by-four right between that jug head's eyes. I'll teach him to leave me stranded.* Well, when I got home. I was steaming. I walked out to the barn, and there stood old Buck. He's standing there with an "It's about time you got home to feed me" look in his eyes. I looked at him, and it was so funny that I rolled on the ground, laughing, and then I got up and fed old Buck.

Top of Coeur d'Alene Mountain where
Old Buck left me to walk home

Mel and Buck

Old Buck   Mel on Buck at Echo Bay farm

THE TICK

I HAD BEEN out all day, riding old Buck, when I got home and went to my room. I took off my dirty jeans, and that's when I found the tick. The tick must have been on old Buck, and he had crawled up and into my pants. Now, I don't know quite how to explain where this tick was. Just let me say that it bored into the lower left quadrant of a very tender spot of the male anatomy. Ouch. Well, Grandma hollered that dinner was ready, and I told her that I was not hungry. So right away, she wanted to know what's wrong with me because I was always hungry. So I told her that I had a tick bored into me, and she said, "Let me see it." I said, "No way, Grandma." She asked where the tick was, and I told her it was in a place that she was not going to see. Finally, she figured out where the tick was and said, "I'll get your grandpa. He is the best tick remover in these parts." So Grandpa came in and said, "Let me look at it." I pulled my shorts down, and Grandpa said, "Ouch." He looked the situation over and said, "Well, the best way to do this is just get a needle red-hot and touch it to that tick's butt, and he will screw himself right out of there." Now, I didn't like the sound of that red-hot needle. I thought of what would happen if, in the heat of the moment, Grandpa's glasses should fog up, and he would miss the tick with that red-hot needle. So Grandpa said, "OK, I will do it the hard way." He got a pair of tweezers and a cold needle and went to work on the tick. He finally got the tick out, and needless to say, I did not ride old Buck for a few days.

FLYING SQUIRREL

WE KIDS GREW up in the woods and around loggers. We all worked in the woods or sawmills at one time or other. Well, one time, we were working in the woods, cutting trees, when we cut this big red fur tree down. When we went to limb it, we found this baby flying squirrel on the ground. We picked him up and took him home. We named him Glider because he would climb up on the curtains and get on top of the window frame. He would dive off the window frame and glide down to a chair or the floor. If someone came over that did not know about Glider, he would glide down and land in their lap, and it would scare the heck out of them. Now, when we were not home, we would put Glider in his cage so he would not be flying and making a mess while we were gone. Well, one day, we were all in a hurry to go somewhere, and we forgot to put Glider in his cage. When we got home, we discovered that Glider was not in his cage, so we started looking for him. We found him. Here's what had happened as near as we could tell. Glider had climbed up the linen closet door and flew into the bathroom. The bad news was someone had left the toilet seat up. Poor old Glider hit the lid and knocked himself out and fell in and drowned. You might say that Glider was canned.

CUTTING WOOD

IT WAS MY thirteenth summer, and there was nothing that I didn't know, and if there was, I thought it probably wasn't worth knowing anyhow. So I was thirteen years old on the farm for the summer. Well, I walked down to the general store. Oh, it was such great place. It was owned by a man; his name was Bill Conkle. He had so much neat stuff in the store. There was a big pot-belly stove in the middle of the store. Out on the porch, he had a World War I machine gun that we kids loved to play with. Well, as I said, I had walked down to the store, and Mr. Conkle asked if I knew how to split wood. So I told old Bill who I felt I was now on the same level with, (you know man to man). "Well, I'm probably the best wood splitter in northern Idaho and maybe all of Idaho." Old Bill said, "Go over and take a look at that wood pile and tell me how much I would charge to split and stack it." Well, I looked it over, went back to the store, and told him, "Shoot, it ain't much wood, but I could do it for two bucks." Bill said, "Are you sure?" And I said, "I hate to charge that much, but you know a first-class wood splitter like me. I can't just give my time away." So Bill said, "Come down in the morning and start on it."

I got up at four in the morning to feed the hogs. I never could figure out why those hogs couldn't eat at seven like everyone else. Down the road to old Bill's store I went. He came out and handed me a nine-pound sledgehammer and a splitting wedge. I looked at him and asked him where his ax was. He said to me, "I don't think you're going to need an ax." You know it's funny how a guy as old as Bill knew so little about splitting wood. Well, I got down to the wood pile, and I don't know how, but that pile got bigger, and the rounds were bigger than they were the day before. So I took a closer look at the wood. It was big old knotty bull pine, not good. I got a round all set up. I took that ax rared back, and *whack*, the ax bounced off. It almost hit me in the head. I was perplexed by this. I thought that maybe I should try that maul-and-wedge thing. Bummer. I thought that I should be done in two hours or less. That day went by pretty slow, and I was about one quarter done. My hands were blistered and shot. I walked three miles home, helped feed them dang hogs, and went to bed. Four in the morning, feeding the dang hogs again. Three miles to the store back to splitting wood. Well, I kept at it for two more days until I was done because Dad told me to never quit, but I was wondering about the wisdom of that statement. Anyway, old Bill gave me five bucks. Cool. As I walked home, it came to my mind that with all I knew about splitting wood, how did I miscalculate that wood pile that badly? Oh well, summer was just getting started. It couldn't get any worse, could it?

AIRPLANES

MY FRIEND ROD Oland and I were up in the attic one day, and we found this old leather flying helmet. It had a radio cord hanging from it. I, being a radio expert at the time, told Rod that we were going to listen to the airplanes. Rod said, "Are you sure that we should do that?" I said, "Sure, trust me. I know what I'm doing." Rod said, "OK." We got a stool and got it under the light in the bathroom. I climbed up on the stool. I took the light bulb out. I put the helmet on, took the radio cord, and stuck it in the light socket. *Wham.* I'm on floor, and Rod is standing over me. He said, "Did you hear the airplanes?" I shook my head and said, "I ain't rightly sure it was an airplane, but I heard something." Rod said, "Let's do it again." I said, "Naw, I'm tired of this radio stuff. Let's go play ringer. You can be it."

RINGER

WE HAD ANOTHER great game. We called it ringer. What we did was to take an old car tire without the rim. All the kids would get on our front porch with the tire. Then whoever was it got on his bike and rode up the road, turned around, and rode as fast as he could. He then had to turn into our yard, and he had to go between the porch and the maple tree. Then the guys on the porch had to try and throw the tire over the rider's head; thus, they made a ringer. But most of the time, they just hit you in the head or upper body. But if you didn't crash, you were the winner, and then you got to go again until you crashed. Then you lose, and the next guy gets his chance to be a winner. It was fun but painful. But we all lived through it and Mom just shook her head and said, "Boys will be boys," and we were.

HORSESHOES

ABOUT A WEEK later after my head quit ringing from my radio work, I thought that I would walk down to the Boy Scout camp. I got down there, and I found Mr. Bill Wood. He was the camp caretaker. So I was talking to old Bill, and he asked me if I played horseshoes. I said, "Heck yes, I am one of if not the best horseshoe player in northern Idaho, maybe in the whole state of Idaho." Old Bill said, "Well, I sure would like to learn how from you, so let's play a game." He told me to go first. Well, I said, "No, you go first." I didn't want to take advantage of an old guy, so I let him go first. Well, old Bill stepped up and threw a ringer—first throw. The score ends up twenty-one to nothing, Bill's favor. It seems to me that he should have told me that he was the one guy in the state of Idaho that was better than me. But he was a gentleman about it and told me that he enjoyed the lesson that I had given him and that he would like to play another game. But I told him, "No thanks. I have hogs to feed."

THE PUMP

AFTER THAT HUMILIATING horseshoe game, I was looking for something that was up to my intelligence level, which was quite high for a thirteen-year-old. Well, Dad found just the thing for me. He said, "Find your brother Doran and go down to the lake and hook up the pump for the garden." Then he said, "Make sure that you check to see that the 220 electric line is turned off before you start hooking it up." All right, something up to my standards because after all, I was one of the best electricians in northern Idaho or maybe the whole state of Idaho. Well, the pump was on a platform in about two feet of water, so I took off my boots and was about to wade in when Doran said, "Dad told you to make sure the power was off." I said, "Naw, I know it's off. Trust me." And he said, "OK." I had that effect on him. I think deep down he knew how brilliant I was. So I was wading knee-deep in the lake. Well, those 220 lines were hanging from a tree branch; just head high to a thirteen-year-old up to his knees in lake water. I ran into those wires on the left side of my head. *Whack.* Next thing I knew, I was floating in the lake with Doran holding my head above water. Then my brother Doran said the most profound thing he has ever said to me. He said, "I don't think the power was off." Well, after the cobwebs went away, we finished hooking up the pump, and we decided Dad did not need to know about this. Dad did want to know why it took so long to hook the pump up. By then, I was back on my game. I said, "You know any job worth doing is worth doing right." Oh, Dad was plum proud of us. I was tired of electrical work, so I took a little time off; besides, I was thinking about flying.

FLYING

A S I SAID, I had been thinking about flying because I knew quite a bit about aeronautics. I was not up to my full potential yet. But the way I first flew had some problems. That was when my whole thirteen years flashed before my eyes in about five seconds, give or take a second or two. I was up on the hill behind the barn. There was a path through the trees; it was about four feet wide with a nice forty-degree slope to it. I told Doran, "This is where we will do it." He said "OK" because that's what little brothers always say to their older, more experienced big brothers. So there are four trees that form a square at the top of the mountain. We cut poles and climbed up ten feet and built a platform, which we called the launching pad. I found out years later that that was a term they used when going to the moon. I was so far ahead of my time. I found two nice springy tamarack trees, about thirty feet downhill from the Launchpad, on each side of the trail. We got a nice, strong rope, one of Dad's favorite ropes; he always wondered what had happened to it. Well, we got a pole that was long enough to reach between the two trees and tied the rope in the middle of the pole. We climbed up the trees with the pole about thirty feet and tied the pole to the trees. Oh, it was a beautiful sight. We got a gunnysack and filled it full of rags and straw. We tied the swing rope in the middle of the sack. We now had equal parts of the sack on both sides of the rope. So here is how it all worked: you would get up on the platform, take hold of the rope, and start pulling back and forth until those two tamarack trees were swaying and about to pull you off the platform. You would jump on the sack, straddle the rope, and launch. If all went well, you flew out about fifty feet from the platform and about twenty feet high—that is, if you went straight down the trail. Otherwise, your flight was cut short and was quite painful. We called it the gungaho sling. One day, Doran came up with a great idea. He said, "What if I get on your shoulders? That way, we will have more weight, and we can fly farther." Now that sounded great, and I was proud that my little brother had taken to this aeronautical stuff so well. It must have been my great teaching ability. Well, up we went; Doran got on my shoulders. We got those trees swaying like never before, and we launched. We went sixty feet out and twenty-five feet high. *Snap*, the rope broke. Now as we glided through the air, this was where my whole life flashed before my eyes. Here we were, twenty-five feet in the air; the rope was hanging straight down, and my brother was on my shoulders—this could not be good. I thought that when we would land, my butt would be where my head used to be. *Crash*, we hit the ground. Doran was OK. I guess I cushioned him with my body. Hey, that's what big brothers do. As for me, I felt shorter for a couple of days. We decided that Mom and Dad did not have to know about this at that time, we thought ten or twelve years later was about the right time to tell them.

ONCE UPON A SUMMER

WELL, AFTER MY flying experience, I was wondering what to do with my life, so I started to look at the many outstanding talents that I had, and let me tell you, there were many. I don't mean to brag, so as Joe Friday said, "Just the facts, ma'am."

I happened to run across a book about the great William Tell. Now, I was not up to reading much at that time because as I mentioned before, there was just not too much that I didn't already know. But this William Tell guy was a man's man. I felt a kindred spirit with a guy like that. So I read it and found that his greatest feat was to put an apple on the head of his friend, take his bow, and split that apple. Now, that right there could make a man great. Well, as I was not a great archery guy at that time—I might add I did become one later on—but at that time, I was the best knife thrower in northern Idaho or maybe in the whole state of Idaho. I thought to myself, *this could work*, so I went looking for my little brother Doran. I found him playing some dumb game in the dirt, and I told him, "You are about to become a legend." He said "OK" because that's what little brothers say to their wiser older brothers. So out behind the barn we went. You know, it seems that a lot of our life was spent out behind the barn. Anyway, I got Doran stood up against the barn wall; I put a two-gallon milk bucket over his head and placed a nice apple on top of the bucket. So I started throwing the knife; it's hitting the bucket, bouncing off and sticking in the barn wall or falling to the ground. For some reason, I was having a hard time hitting that apple. Just when I was about to become famous, our mother came around the corner of the barn and yelled out, "What are you doing?" I said, "I'm going to split that apple on Doran's head." She said, "No, you are going to kill your little brother." And with that, she disarmed me and kept Doran from becoming a legend in his own time. I decided that I would have to get better with my bow and arrow because you never know when you will have a chance to be great.

THE LONG SWIM

WELL, LIKE I said, I was working on becoming a world-class archer, so I was down by the lake, all by myself. I had done some of my best stuff by myself, but this did not happen to be one of those times. I shot at a stump, but I missed it—must have been the wind. Anyway, the arrow went out into the lake. I thought to myself, *it's not too far out. I will just swim out and get it.* As for swimming, I had just advanced above the dog paddle stage, but I still used the dog paddle just for fun. Anyway as I said, I was swimming out to get my arrow. I reached for it and missed, and it floated a little farther out. I swam out and tried again. I missed, and the arrow floated out farther. After about four tries, I got the arrow and turned to go back. Dang, I was a long way from shore. I started swimming, and I was not getting anywhere fast. This was another one of those times when my life flashed before my eyes. I couldn't go any farther—even my dog paddle was pooped out. As I went down for the third time, my feet hit the bottom. I pushed up and got a breath, went down again, pushed up, and got a breath. Anyway, I kept doing this until I reached the shore. Guess what? I still had my arrow. I might have swum better without it, but it was one of my best ones. I thought to myself, *No one knows about this, and if they did, they might cramp my style and tell me not to go near the lake alone.* But there was just too much neat stuff to explore. So I thought sixty years was about right to tell this story, so now you have it.

MEAN KID

ABOUT THIS TIME, we had a big kid that lived somewhere, but he would come to our street and whip up on us. Well, this was starting to chap my butt real bad, so I came up with a plan. Hey, that's what big brothers do. So I called the gang together and explained the plan to them. We knew when this kid came by every day, so I told them to all be on the porch at that time. I went in the house and got Mom's broom and hid in the big bush by the telephone pole at the front of our place by the road. Well, at four thirty sharp, here came the big dude, so my guys started hollering stuff at him—you know, stuff like, "Your mother wears combat boots" and "Did your parents have any kids that lived?" and "Your feet stinks, and you don't love Jesus" or "If brains were dynamite, you wouldn't have enough to blow your nose." Well, you know that this enraged this stupid big kid—just what we wanted. He was yelling that he was going to beat us all bad and that we just had to come out in the street. He turned around and started past our place again. So out of the bush I came. I took that broomstick and ran it through the front spokes on his bike. Jazam, it took every spoke out, and down he went. Off the porch came all those little guys. They jumped on him. They whipped him pretty good. The guy went down the street, dragging his bike, snot coming out of his nose, and he was crying. I tell you, it was the most beautiful sight any of us had ever seen. The kid never came back. He must have found another way to go home.

THE BAT

DORAN AND I were out in the yard, and all of a sudden, a bat came flying around. Cool. So I thought that that bat would make a really cool pet. We grabbed a fishnet that was hanging on the barn wall, and the chase was on. That little sucker dived at us and away from us, but two great white hunters like us would never give up. Finally, the bat swooped the wrong way, and with a mighty swing of the net, we caught him. Now that we had him on the ground, we looked into the eyes of the ugliest thing we had ever seen in our lives—little beady eyes and an ugly mouth with lots of teeth. I asked Doran, "You want him for a pet?" He said, "Not me." Well, I sure didn't want the ugly little sucker, so we did the only thing we could; we stomped the snot out of him, which was good except we bent Grandpa's fishing net. But that was OK because they were so happy that we were not bitten by the bat because if a bat is flying around at high noon, he most likely has rabies, and they all thought we were crazy enough anyway.

THE SHOOTING

ONE DAY, DORAN and I had been shooting our BB gun, and we were out of BBs. We're sitting on the porch, trying to figure out what to do with the rest of our day. Well, our younger brother, whom you have not met yet but are about to, was coming across the street. So I came up with a great idea. I told Doran, "We are out of BBs. The gun's empty, so just cock the gun and aim at Gordy and pull the trigger. He will think that we're shooting at him." So Doran cocked the gun, aimed at our little brother, and pulled the trigger. Gordy fell down on the road, moaning and rolling around, so we ran over to see what's going on. Guess what? There was one BB left in the gun. It hit him right between the eyes, just above his nose, and made a big old welt. We told Gordy that we thought that it was best for him to tell Mom and Dad that he got hit with a stick instead of the fact that we shot him. He's OK, still has twenty-twenty vision, but he does get kind of jumpy if he sees Doran or me with a gun. You would think that after fifty years that he would get over it.

THAT PIG VERONICA

WELL, LIKE I said, we raised about four hundred hogs year-round, so I thought you should hear a few pig stories. Well, first off, we had a forty-foot-by-one-hundred-foot barn, and it was divided into pens that were twelve feet wide and sixteen feet long. Each pen would hold twenty pigs. Once you put those twenty pigs into that pen, you cannot add any other pigs, or the pigs in the pen will chew up the new one and kill it. I told you all of this to tell you about Veronica. She was just another pig until the day she got out of her pen and into another pen. When Doran and I went out to feed the hogs in the morning, we found her, and she was chewed up and in bad shape. We got her out of the pen and took her to the farrowing barn; it also was our hog hospital. We started nursing her back to health. We cleaned her cuts up and poured disinfectant on them and gave her a big shot of Tyramicin. She got better in a few days, and that's when we noticed something funny. Her ear was broken and hung down over her eye. I was watching an old movie. I saw an actress that had her hair hanging over one eye and I thought that's Veronica, and that's how our pig got her name. Well, Veronica had free reign from then on. She followed us around like a dog. Then one night, she got into another pen, and yep, she got chewed up again. Well, we got her well again, and we just called her stupid, and we sold her.

CHESTER AND THE GREAT ESCAPE

I REMEMBER ONE time we were moving our big old boar Chester and two of our sows from one barn to another one about five miles down the road. Well, we got to the barn and backed up to the loading ramp. Guess what? We didn't have any hogs in the truck. Somehow, old Chester had gotten the tailgate open, and they had jumped out somewhere. Well, we went looking for them, and we found them down off the road, rooting around in Rock Creek. We got the two sows headed home but not old Chester; he wasn't moving, so we went ahead and got the two sows home and in the barn. Doran and I were wondering how we were going to get old Chester home before Dad found out that we had lost him. Then I remembered that an old man had told me once that if you put a rope on the hind leg of a pig, you could lead them anywhere you wanted to. If I ever see that old man again, I would tie a rope to him, and it won't be around his leg. So we gave Chester time to relax and settle down at the creek bottom. Doran and I snuck down the creek bank, and we found old Chester sound asleep, right in the middle of a big old serviceberry bush. Now, the serviceberry bush has thorns about an inch long on all its branches. It has purple berries on it that are full of seeds and taste like reused bubble gum. (Icky) Back to the mission at hand; we crawled up to Chester, and I talked softly to him. He just grunted and let me put the rope around his back leg. Now, let me tell you about Chester; he weighed seven hundred pounds and did anything he wanted whenever he wanted to. So after I got the rope on his hind leg, I motioned for Doran to do his part. Well, Doran had a six-battery cattle prod with him that must have put out about six bazillion volts. I got a good grip on the rope. By that, I mean it's wrapped around my hand tight. I nodded my head, and Doran poked old Chester in the butt with the prod and pushed the button. Chester jumped and pulled me right through that serviceberry bush, and he then proceeded to lead me anywhere he wanted to go, and it sure wasn't to the barn. I thought it was supposed to be the other way around. I finally got loose from the rope, and after I got all the thorns out of my body and the bleeding stopped, I started to think seriously about shooting old Chester. I went to get the tractor, and we went down to the creek. We got a rope around Chester right behind his front legs, and I pulled him all the way to the barn and put him back in with the sows. Dad got home and asked if we had any trouble moving Chester and the sows. I said, "Heck no. After all, I am the best hog mover in northern Idaho." Then Dad said, "How come you have all of those Band-Aids on?" I said, "Well, I was busy picking serviceberries and fell into the bush." Dad said, "Sometimes, son, I don't think you are too bright. I send you out to move some hogs around, and you waste your time picking serviceberries." Well, I went out in the morning, and danged, if old Chester wasn't graveyard dead. I told Dad, "Dang, that move must have been hard on old Chester." Dad said, "Yeah, because I know you boys took good care of him on the move over here, right?"

THE HOSE JOB

THIS IS ABOUT one of our breed sows that had a slight problem. When she was little, she got stepped on, and her tail was gone, and her rear end was somewhat rearranged. But she went on to be one of our better sows. She always had big litters and cared for her babies quite well. We were building a new barn for all our sows. So we had moved our sows into another barn that had a concrete floor, and we had put wood chips on the floor for bedding. Oh, by the way, her name was Jennifer. She was a Landrace. OK, let me explain that. The Landrace pigs were from England. Originally, they were bred to have one more rib than any other pig. This means that they were longer, and that means more bacon on them than most other hogs. So one day, Jennifer started to look like she was not feeling well, so Doran and I started keeping a close eye on her. Well, we came out one morning, and we saw right away that Jennifer was down and sick. Dad was gone, out on the road somewhere on farm business. So it's just Mom and us boys at home. We got together, and I finally figured out what was wrong with Jennifer. We were feeding the sows in the old barn with the wood chips on the floor. Well, when they dropped food on the floor, they would pick it up and eat it—sawdust and all. This did not bother the other sows, but as I said, Jennifer had that rear-end-alignment problem. So I figured out that those wood chips were not making the full trip through poor old Jennifer. Now I was smart enough to know that she was in bad shape. If I didn't do something, she was not going to make it. So after a great amount of thinking, here's what I came up with: I told Mom, Doran, and Gordon my plan, and Mom said, "Well, it worked on you kids, so let's give it a try, but how are we going to do it?" First off, Doran and I got Jennifer up on her feet, and we got ropes around her body and got her tied to the barn wall so she could not lie down on us. Then I told Mom to get in front and watch Jennifer and let me know how she was doing. Now we get to the delicate part. I don't know quite how to put this, but here it goes. I took the garden hose and moved around behind Jennifer, and how shall I say it? I placed the hose in just the right spot. Then I told Doran to turn it on, and he did. I forgot about having sixty pounds of water pressure. All of a sudden, Mom hollered, "She is turning purple, and her eyes are bugging out real bad." So I did the only thing I could. Yep, I pulled the hose out. Now, old Jennifer painted me and the barn with green sawdust and other things too gross to mention. But you know that it got Jennifer back to feeling well, and we just kept her away from sawdust after that. You might say that everything came out OK.

THE CANNON

ANOTHER TIME IN the woodshop, Ted and I thought that we should make a gun to shoot marbles. We had an eighteen-inch-long-by-half-inch-wide water pipe. Then we cut the body of our cannon out of oak when the teacher wasn't looking. We needed a piece of steel to hook the barrel to. I had hiked over to the dump on my way home from school the day before. I found a three-inch-by-six-inch-by-half-inch flat bar—just right. I took it to school the next day. Ted thought it would work fine. One problem was we needed two holes drilled in the plate. We needed the two holes on each side of the pipe so that we could use the U-bolt that I had found at the dump. You ask how I got into the dump. Well, when I was a kid, a dump was a real dump. People just drove in and dumped stuff over the hill, and it was fair game for anyone to pick through. Some of the best rat hunting I ever did was at the dump. But that is another story that I will save for later. Anyway, the dump was not a sanitary landfill like they have today. Shoot, I would go to the dump with Grandpa and come home with more stuff then we went with. People just threw away too much good stuff. Well, back to our cannon. We had to drill the two holes, so we had our other good friend Don to stand watch for the teacher to make sure he did not see us drilling metal on the shop's drill press. We had to drill our holes quickly, so there was no time for a vise to hold our work. So I told Ted, "I can hold it, OK? You just drill it." Well, I could not hold it, and as the drill bit, grabbed hold, and started spinning the metal, it hit my thumb. I still have the scar today. We got the drill press shut down, and I whipped into the bathroom and started trying to stop the bleeding with paper towels. I finally got the bleeding stopped. And we got all the towels stuffed into the trash can. We never got caught and never got that cannon done dang it. But you want to know what the saddest part is when you drive by the old dump. They covered it with dirt and made a water park out of it. It brings a tear to my eye every time I go past on the freeway that used to be the field that was my entry to the best dump in the world.

UNDERWATER

I REMEMBER ONE time when I came up with a great idea on how to make some cash. When I got to school, I started telling the guys what a great swimmer I was. They all said, "Yeah, right." So I told them that I was the best swimmer in northern Idaho and maybe the whole state of Idaho. To which they all threw up their hands and started to walk away. I then said that I was so good that I could stay underwater for half an hour with no problem. They stopped, turned around, and said, "No way." I said, "Yes, I can stay underwater for as long as I want to." To which they said, "You mean you can stay all the way underwater for as long as you want to?" I said, "Yep, but I am not going to do it for nothing. But I will bet you guys a dollar each that I can do it." So I got ten guys to bet me. They all wanted to know when I was going to do this. I said, "Right now." I led them all into the bathroom. I filled the sink full of water and climbed down under the sink and sat on the floor and under the water. Well, these guys were real mental giants, and it took them a minute or two to figure out that they had been had. I was just sitting there with my hand out for the money. The guys were making so much noise that the principal who happened to be walking down the hall heard them. He walked in, saw me under the sink, shook his head, and said, "Melvin, what are you doing under the sink?" Well, before I could say anything, the guys started telling him how I was cheating them out of their lunch money. "So what's the deal, Melvin?"

"Well, I bet these guys a dollar each that I could stay underwater as long as I wanted to, and here I am." The principle said, "Melvin, your time underwater is up, and you are not taking these boys' money. I will see you after school because I think you are probably the best chalk-eraser cleaner in the whole school. Lord knows you get enough practice."

HEAT ADVISORY

YOU SEE THE TV news, and they have a heat advisory: everyone is going to die because it might be one hundred degrees today. How did we ever survive? You know how? We took our clothes off, put our swimsuits on, and went running through the sprinkler or went to the pool or the lake. Our elders sat in the shade and watched us kids running around in the heat. *We* were riding our bikes, playing games, sitting in the shade, and yes, drinking from that old rubber garden hose. Of course, Mom always had that great Kool-Aid mixed up for us. You know, that drink mix that was one pack of Kool-Aid, one quart of water, and last but not least, two big cups of *sugar*. We did not need anyone telling us it was hot out. Guess what? We knew it was summertime and it was hot. That's what we waited all winter for. No one that I knew ever died from summertime heat and we soaked up all the heat we could before winter came again.

HOOKY BOBBING

I WAS THE best hooky bobber in northern Idaho and maybe in the whole state of Idaho. What is hooky bobbing you ask? It happens in the wintertime. It is such a great sport that I think it should be in the Winter Olympics. It is dangerous and takes great skill to perform. Here is how we did it: You would find a good intersection where cars had to stop. You had to pick a spot that had good cover to hide behind so that the driver and your parents could not see you. This was best done in the dark as it is always colder and easier to hide. Here is how you hooky bobbed: You waited for a car to come along and stop at the stop sign. Oh, I forgot; you need to hide on the passenger side of the road so that the driver can't see you. You have to be quick because the car won't be stopped for long. You come out from cover and stay low so that you are not seen in the rearview mirror. You would crouch down and grab hold of the bumper and hang on and let the car pull you until you are going too fast to keep your feet under you, then you let go. When you stop sliding, you go back, hide, and wait for another car. I just remembered one time when we were out hooky bobbing. My brother Doran was not too tall at the time. He was too short to crouch down, so he would stand up straight and grab the bumper. One day, Doran got hooked up, and the guy driving put the hammer down. Doran was going faster than he had ever gone before. We kept yelling for him to let go. His legs were shaking, and we knew that he couldn't hold on much longer. He finally did let go, and he spun around, did a backward flip, slid into a ditch, and backed out again and came up on his feet. Now, that right there would score a perfect ten in the Olympics if they had hooky bobbing like they should have.

I had a great plan for hooky bobbing, but as I have said before, it was the best laid plans of mice and men. Well, here is how my great plan worked: We had a great sleigh-riding hill. It did happen to be a public road, so there were cars bugging us all the time. So I called the gang together and explained my plan to them. Of course, they thought it was brilliant—how could it be anything else coming from me? What we would do was get two kids to a sled. One kid would steer, and the other one would crouch on the back of the sled. When a car would come by, they would shove off on the sled. The front guy would steer up alongside the car, and the guy on the back of the sled would grab the bumper and goes hooky bobbing. Cool. All went well until one day when Eddie and I were teamed up on a sled. A car came by, and we were after it. Eddie was having a hard time steering in close enough, but he finally got close. Just as I went to make the transfer, Eddie hit a rut and went in to the tire, which sucked the sled up into the fender; well, it was a bad noise. The driver got the car stopped and jumped out. He thought that he had run over a sled and killed someone. When he found out that he had not killed anyone, he pulled the sled out of the fender well and gave us ten bucks and beat feet. So I guess my plan worked OK. We bought candy for all of us for a week with the ten bucks. Not bad.

MELVIN BROWN

THE BIG SAUCER

DORAN AND I were down at Nick's junk emporium, looking around for a used sled. Now, Nick did not have many shelves in his shop, and if he did, we never could find them. Nick was a "look at it and feel it and buy it" kind of guy. We kids could spend hours, looking and listening to Old Nick as he told us about all the priceless stuff in his shop. But you know, with all the priceless stuff he had, it seemed like everything we picked out always had a price on it. It must have been that Nick really liked us because most of the stuff we picked out was stuff we thought was priceless. But Old Nick would put a price on it just so we could buy it. Nick would have a tear in his eye because he had to let one of his priceless things go just to make two little boys happy. Anyway, we were looking through this big stack of stuff when I spied a red something sticking out of the pile. Doran and I got hold of it and pulled it out of the pile. It was an old metal Coca-Cola sign; it was six feet across and concave. I looked at it and said, "This is it. This will be the ultimate snow saucer." I did not want to let Nick know how bad we wanted the saucer. After all, you know what great deals I have made in the past. So I was ready to deal with Nick. When he said, "Five bucks," I said, "OK." So we got Dad to haul our saucer home in the truck. We took that saucer, turned it over, and waxed it up with paraffin wax that Mom used for canning. We got Loran, Jim, Doran, Jenkins, and me. We could all get into the saucer at the same time. Well, we rode it on some small hills, and it went really fast, so we figured we were ready for the hill. The hill was out behind the barn, of course. Where else would it be? The hill was on a ridge. One side led down into the big hay field and was free of any obstacles that might kill us. The other side, however, was very steep for about one hundred yards, and then there was the barbwire fence and then the trees. This is not the side of the hill to sled down on. The ridge is narrow, and you had to make sure you went down the correct side of the hill. We got all set up to go. Everyone was in the saucer except Jenkins. He jumped in, and he jarred the saucer, and it went over the wrong side of the hill. Now, it seemed we were going a hundred miles an hour. I don't think it was quite that fast, but it felt like it. The saucer would spin around, and you would see the barn, then you would see the fence and the trees. Around and around we went. Now my life was starting to flash before my eyes again. I just hate that. So I hollered, "Bail out, boys." Well, Loran was the first one out. He hit the snow, and for a minute, he was going faster than the saucer, then all of a sudden, he found a hidden bale of hay or something and stopped immediately. Jim hollered, "See ya, boys," and out he went. When he hit the snow, his feet went straight up in the air, and he kicked Jenkins in the head, and then he was gone. Well, Jenkins fell out of the saucer and tumbled over and over, then his feet hit the ground, and he went straight up in the air. He could have won a world high-jump competition. Then there was just Doran and I left in the saucer, and we were closer to the fence and those trees than ever. I tried to grab hold of Doran as I bailed out of the saucer, but I missed, and just as I hit the snow, I saw Doran in the middle of the saucer, hunkered down on the bottom. I slid right up to the fence and stopped with the aid of a fence post. Ouch. Well, Doran and the saucer were thin enough to go under the bottom wire on the fence unharmed. We all jumped up and hobbled down to save my brother. We figured that he was wrapped around a tree as we didn't see him right away. Well, he went right between two trees and ended up in a pile of pucker brush about two feet off the ground. He was sitting in the saucer when we found him, and here is what Doran said: "Dang that was great. Let's do it again." We all thought that we should have beaten him to within an inch of his life just so he could see how much fun the rest of us had. But what the heck we all had a great story to tell, and ain't that what life's all about?

WILD CAR RIDE

I HAVE HAD some wild car rides in my time. I am going to tell you of the time I went for a ride with my aunt Elaine. My aunt Elaine is the craziest, greatest, most fun aunt anyone could have. She is now ninety-one years old and still more fun than people half her age. Well, I was about eight years old, and we were on vacation on the Washington coast. This is where my Aunt Elaine and uncle Gordy live. They have two daughters, Claudia and Paula, and a son, David. I love them all very much and love to spend time with them whenever I can. Well, anyway, we were all going out to Camino Island to do some clam digging. Dad and Uncle Gordy decided to rent a rowboat. Aunt Elaine was going to go out for a little boat ride with them. She went out onto the dock with Paula in her arms and went to step into the boat. It moved, and she fell in the water. But she kept Paula above water, laughing the whole time. There was never a dull moment with Aunt Elaine around. We spent the whole day there, and then it was time to go. Elaine was going to drive Mom and all us kids home, and that's where it all started. As I said, I was eight years old and fearless. Anyway, that's what I thought until the ride. When we came down to the beach, it was a steep narrow gravel lane, so we had to go back up that steep narrow gravel lane. Aunt Elaine and my mom got all of us kids stuffed into the backseat of her 1947 fluid drive Plymouth, and off we went. She got about halfway up the hill, and it wouldn't go any farther. All Aunt Elaine said was "Hang on, kids." She put it in reverse, and down the hill we went and she never looked back. She just backed down the hill, laughing all the way down. While, Aunt Elaine was laughing I was about to pee in my pants. She said, "Hang on, kids." And up the hill we went again. We almost made it that time. That old fluid drive must have run out of fluid. So once again she said, "Hang on, kids," and back we went. We got to the bottom. We stopped just short of the ocean. Aunt Elaine said again, "Hang on, kids." And with a mighty roar, we made it to the top of the hill. Funny thing was that Elaine's kids never were scared. It was just another ride with their mom.

CHILI AND CLAMS

AFTER THE CAR ride, we got back to Uncle Gordon's cabin on Lake Ki. We started cleaning the geoduck clams, and Aunt Elaine and Mom started a big old pot of chili. When we got the clams all cleaned, we cut them up and started making clam chowder. When everything was cooked, we had about two gallons of chili and two gallons of clam chowder. There were ten of us there, and we ate all the chili and chowder. I mentioned that this was Uncle Gordon's cabin. Now, when I say cabin, if small comes to mind, you would be right. This cabin was about thirteen by thirteen feet, and we were all going to sleep in the cabin that night. We all got our sleeping bags and started jockeying for a position. One tried to not get pinned in a corner. Now the lights went out, and we all settled down, and then it started. You would hear a strange sound and a giggle from somewhere in the room. But no one knew where it came from because it was dark. And then another one came from somewhere else in the room. Now, this went on half of the night. The air was becoming stale, and you could not put your head into your own sleeping bag because it had become toxic also. But we all lived through it, and we decided that chili and clam chowder don't mix so well. But we have laughed about it for some forty years whenever we all got together. I like that. I think too many families don't have enough to laugh about together.

STRAWBERRY FIELDS FOREVER

WELL, MY GRANDFATHER Brown owned a strawberry farm on the Washington coast. I decided that I would go over there for the summer and make my fortune by picking strawberries. Yes, I was still looking to make my fortune because the market for farts had dried up. So I thought, why not pick strawberries? After all, I know the owner. How bad could it be? On the first day, the picking crew showed up early in the morning. There were old people, young people, men, women, girls, and boys. Well, I figured I would be working with my grandpa. Grandpa took me aside and told me that I would be part of the picking crew and old Henry there would be my boss. I said, "OK." So old Henry took me aside and said, "You ever pick strawberries for a living before?" I said, "Nope, but I'm sure you will spend some time explaining how." Old Henry said, "It ain't going to take that long." Then he pointed up at the sun and asked me if I knew what it was. Now by this time, I was not too impressed with old Henry. I said, "Heck yes, I know what that is. It's the sun." Henry said, "Good. Now, you just point your butt at the sun, put your head between your legs, and pick anything that's red." OK, I could do that. No problem. Well, I did just what old Henry told me to do. I was picking away. I looked up, and the picking crew was gone. They were clear down at the other end of the strawberry patch. They must not be picking as clean as I was. I looked over at their rows, and I didn't see anything red left behind. I looked back at my row, and I did miss one or two berries, and I wondered how that happened. Well, I picked all day by myself because the rest of the crew were so far ahead of me that I could barely see them. At the end of the day, I think I made about a buck and a half. I heard the crew talking. Most of them made fifteen dollars each. One old woman who looked like she might have been a hundred years old said she made seventeen dollars. Now that hurt right there. At this rate, it's going to take me about fifty years to get rich—not good. After three days, Grandpa took me aside and said, "Melvin, I have been watching you pick strawberries for three days now, and I have come to a business decision. I need to get you out of the strawberry patch while I still have one." He said, "I have decided to make you a weights-and-measure man and tractor driver." All right, I knew it would not take Grandpa long to see what great potential I had. So basically, I would drive the tractor to the field and weigh the strawberry flats, credit the picker for his work, and drive back to the barn. You might say that I became Grandpa's right-hand man. I am not sure everyone else would say that, but I have never been shy about saying how good I actually am. Well, just like that, strawberry season was over, so I was off to Idaho because I knew my other grandpa needed me to help him run the ranch. I think I was just too important to be gone too long. You know, it is tough to be in such demand, but I did my best because that's the kind of guy I am.

BACK TO SCHOOL

S UMMER WAS OVER; back to school I am now in the sixth grade. We met our new teacher. He looked at me like he wanted to say "I have been waiting for you." Now he and I had crossed paths throughout my educational career, but this was the first time he had me as a student. I use the term *student* loosely, and I think my teacher did as well. Mr. Joe was one of the best teachers I ever had. He had never heard the saying, "Cut me some slack." He was over six feet tall; to me, he looked eight feet tall. He could be writing on the blackboard with his back to the class. One of us, usually I, would have something really important to whisper to Ted, Don, or Loran. Mr. Joe could swing around and hit me with a piece of chalk like it had been shot from a gun. Shut me right up well for a little while anyway, but there was just too much to talk about. One day, I guess Mr. Joe was having a hard day because I was having a private talk with Ted. All of a sudden, I saw Ted's eyes get big, and I looked around, and Mr. Joe was standing right behind me—not good. He said to me, "Melvin, I want you to get your desk and follow me." I grabbed my desk, and we went out into the hall. He then told me to sit out there in the hall until I could quit talking, and he went back into the classroom. I was all alone in the hallway except for all the people that came by and said, "Melvin, what are you doing out here in the hallway?" So I sat out there for four periods. Finally, Mr. Joe came out and said, "Melvin, do you think you can behave yet?" I looked at him and said, "I don't know, and I sure don't want to make a mistake." He looked at me and said, "Get your desk, and get back into the room, and I suggest that you try very hard to get on my good side." I thought to myself, *Man, this is going to be a great story to tell.*

BIKE RIDES

WELL, I WAS the best bicycle rider in northern Idaho or maybe the whole state of Idaho and even all of eastern Washington. So here are some of my best bike stories. When I got my first bike, I think I was about five years old. Dad would get me going and let go. I could ride it OK, but I did not quite understand all I knew about coaster brakes. What, you ask, are coaster brakes? I know this is hard to believe, but we did not have hand brakes with those little rubber things that rub on your tire rims to stop you. No, we had man-sized brakes. They had man-sounding names like New Departure. This is what happened to you if the bolt on your brake arm fell out: When you pushed back on the pedal to stop, the brake arm would come forward, and you would depart from your bike—not good. Before I learned how to brake, the best way for me to stop was to run into Mr. McLean's Model T Ford pickup, which was parked at the house next door. It worked OK, but Mom got tired of bandaging me up all the time. You know, I see these kids nowadays with their bike helmets and flak jackets and leg guards. They look like something from outer space. If I had worn all that stuff, I would never have been able to do all the great tricks that you are going to read about here. Mom told my dad that he had to teach me how to use my brakes. Well, after learning how to use my brakes, my tires did not last too long. Man, I could slide the tires and skid all the way around and make that gravel fly. I was on my way to becoming a great cyclist.

I got my dare devil tricks from my grandpa Lewis. Check out his bike

Mel and his bike. Check out the old garbage truck.

Mel and Doran in front of the Woodruf house in Spokane.

THE PENNY LOAFER KICK

AS I GOT older and better at bike riding, I started coming up with ways to be great. One of these stories comes to mind. I guess I was about twelve years old at the time. Ah, my buddies loved this trick that I had perfected. I could be riding my bike and kick my penny loafer off. What? You don't know what a penny loafer is? Well, it is a slip-on shoe that had a piece of leather with a slit cut in it and was sown on to the tongue. In this slit, you would place a shiny penny. Ah, it was way cool. Well, anyway, I could kick my penny loafer up in the air and reach out and catch it and put it back on my foot and keep right on riding my bike. One day, I was riding with the gang, and they were begging me to do my famous shoe trick. OK, I kicked my shoe off, and I kicked it out a little too far. I reached out to catch it. I missed and hit the front wheel with my hand. I went over the handlebars, and down on the pavement I went. I ripped the leg of my jeans, and my leg looked kind of like hamburger. My buddies got me home, and my mother came out. She wanted to know what happened. I started telling Mom how I had this terrible bike accident that definitely was not my fault. My story seemed to vary a great deal from the story my buddies were telling her. My mother looked at me and said, "You kicked your shoe up in the air and tried to catch it, and you missed and crashed. Yes or no?" I gave my mother my best "you don't trust me" look and then said yes. My mother then pulled my pants off in front of all my buddies and took her bottle of iodine out. Now my leg looked like hamburger. As she rubbed that iodine in, I was writhing around in great pain. My buddies were laughing their heads off, and as a famous man once said, "I don't get no respect." Well, after that humiliating scene, I did not do the penny loafer trick too much but every once in a while I did it, just to show that I still had it. I would perform it for my friends while riding my bike but only on the grass. I only did the trick if my mother was not around.

THE VALLEY OF DOOM

ANOTHER TRICK THAT I perfected was riding my bike like a horse. You ask how this trick can be done. Well, it might be hard for the average guy to do. But we are not talking average here. We're talking about me. Here's how I did it. I don't know how many of you remember what the old Schwinn handlebars looked like. If you turned them upside down, they turned down and came straight back toward you. I took the handgrips off and then took a rawhide shoelace. I put the end through the hole of the handgrip and tied a big knot in the lace so it would stay in the handgrip. I did this in both handgrips and put them back on the handlebars. I now had reins just like you would ride a horse with. I was great at riding my bike with no hands anyway, so this was easy for me. I would just steer with my reins. I could go anywhere I wanted to. Well, one day, the gang and I were over at the high school. We were there because it was summertime and the pool where we swam a lot was open. So we were riding around, doing great things on our bikes. Well, we had a couple of new guys that were riding with us. I don't know where they came from. They just started riding around with us. Now, we were a pretty tight group, so we wanted some proof that these two guys were good enough to ride with us. Someone said, "Let's go ride the Valley of Doom." Right away, these two guys wanted to know what the Valley of Doom was. Well, naturally, they left it up to me to explain. "Well, guys, we don't know how good you are or think you are, so we will let the Valley of Doom sort it out for us." So these two guys said, "Oh, yeah, let us at it because we are the best bike riders in these parts." Now, the Valley of Doom is behind the school. It is a paved loading ramp that goes down to the basement's loading doors. It is fourteen feet wide and has cement walls on both sides of the driveway. Here's what you had do: You would ride into the valley and go down, and just before you got to the doors, you hit your brakes and did a sliding turn. If you did everything right, you ended up stopped sideways to the doors, and you beat the grim reaper. If you did it wrong, that's when you met the Doors of Doom.

After explaining all of this to the new guys, I asked, "Which one of you is going to go first?" They looked at each other and said, "We would like you to go first." I said, "Why me?"

"Because you are the expert here, and we need to see how you do it." Then the rest of the guys said, "Yeah, we want to see you ride your horse bike into the Valley of Doom." Sometimes there's no way out for a leader, so I said, "OK." I got to the top of the ramp, grabbed hold of my reins, and down I went. I got to where I had to hit my brakes and turn my handlebars. I hit the brakes hard, and I pulled hard on the left rein, and the handgrip came off. Now this meant that I was now pulling hard on the right handgrip, which turned the front wheel into the Doors of *Doom*. I hit hard. It threw me into the doors. As I slid along the doors, I hit the cement wall and ended up on top of my bike at the foot of the Doors of Doom. The guys ran down and helped get me up, and they checked me out. Outside of a few puncture wounds and scrapes and bruises, I was in fine shape for the shape I was in. The two new guys were standing at the top, looking down at us. So by this time, I was almost back to normal, and I asked them, "Which one of you wants go first?" Next thing we knew, those two guys were on their bikes, and they were gone. I guess some guys are just not cut out to ride in the Valley of Doom.

BOTTLES AND BIKES

I AM GOING to give you some Idaho and Washington history that most of you would never know if it weren't for me. You see, back when we were kids, the state of Washington shut all its bars on Sundays—no booze. On the other hand, the state of Idaho's bars were open every day including Sunday. Now, the Idaho state line is only ten miles from the city of Spokane, Washington, and the main highway to Idaho went straight through the state-line village on the Idaho side. Now, I am going to tell you about the upstanding state-line village. Where should I start? Let's see, there was the First and Last Chance Bar. They had a wooden Indian with a loincloth on him, and if someone lifted the loincloth, red lights and horns went off, and it was usually a woman who lifted the cloth—embarrassing. Then there was Hard Luck Charles Bar. Then there was the Kontiki Bar. Then there was the State Line Gardens Bar. That was all there was there. These bars were only ten miles from two hundred thousand thirsty people that were dry on Sundays. This is where Ted and I came up with a way to get rich. I know what you're thinking, but this time, we could not miss. We would be rich. Here was our plan: we knew that all the cars coming from the state line back to Spokane had to get rid of their empty beer bottles because the Washington State Patrol were patrolling heavily on Sundays.

Ted and I started early on Monday morning, riding our bikes ten miles to the state line, finding bottles all along the way. We turned around at the line and started back down the other side of the highway, finding bottles along the way. We had bottles hanging from the handlebars in bags and six-pack boxes that we found along the way. We had about a hundred bottles as we rode toward the Safe Way Store to cash in and make our fortune. As we rode along, we got pretty close to each other, and then all of a sudden, our handlebars locked together. Down we went. Oh, it was a terrible noise. We did not get cut at all, but we broke almost all our bottles and went away broke again.

DEAD MAN CREEK

WE LIKED TO take our fishing poles and bikes and ride eight miles to Dead Man Creek. I don't know how it got that name, but it always made us nervous when we camped overnight. As you know, there are strange things that come out of the water at night. Well, Bob and I rode out to the creek and sat about, fishing. You already know that I was the best fisherman in northern Idaho and maybe the whole state of Idaho. Anyway, I had just put a big old night crawler on my best eagle claw worm hook and threw it out into the creek. I was fishing with a telescoping all-steel eagle claw pole when all of a sudden, my pole almost bent, which in those days meant whatever was on the line was big. It had to have been big to bend a telescoping steel eagle claw pole. I started fighting this fish. We went down the creek, and then we went up the creek. I went on fighting this fish until I was all worn out. He was about to take all my line, which was not too hard to do because I only had about twenty yards of line. I finally started to gain on this monster. I knew it was going to be the biggest fish ever taken from Dead Man Creek. All of a sudden, this fish started toward shore, and I told Bob to get ready to grab that sucker. Then I saw Bob backing up. I wondered why when up the bank came the ugliest, meanest, bad-assed snapping turtle I had ever seen. He was not about to let me take that hook out, not that I wanted to, so we cut him loose and let him chase us to our bikes. You know, I would have mounted him for a trophy but somehow I don't think he would have let me nail him to a board.

BOOM

REMEMBER, THIS STORY happened back when boys could still make things go boom. Well, Larry and I had an old used CO2 cylinder, so we thought we would see if we could make it go boom. Here is what we did. Now I had done things that people said were plum stupid, but I did not agree with them most of the time. But this was plum stupid, if I do say so myself. We took the cylinder, which had been punctured, so the CO2 was gone. We drilled the soft plug out in the end of the cylinder. We then took a twelve-gauge shotgun shell apart and got the gunpowder from it. We then poured the gunpowder into the cylinder until it was half-full. Then we cut the heads off wooden matches. We stuffed them into the cylinder until the main body was full. Now, this was all bad enough. If the matches had ignited, it would not have been good, but so far so good. You are talking about two mental giants here. That would be Larry and me. We had to find a way to seal the end up. We finally came up with a great plan. Well, it seemed like it at the time, but as I look back on it, it was not so great. What we did was put some cotton down on the match heads and then soldered the end shut. Now we had the bomb done, but we forgot one thing: we had no way to set it off. We put our heads together as we sat on the back porch. All of a sudden, it came to us. As we sat there, we smelled that wonderful smell that we all loved so much: the burning barrel. You see, every house had a burning barrel in the backyard. There was no use hauling paper to the dump; just burn it along with whatever else you had that would burn. You could have half a dozen burn barrels burning all at the same time usually after dark. There were two reasons for this: one was that the fire department would not see where the fire was, and two was that you could see where you started little spot fires in the neighborhood, but it was no problem because everyone had their hoses out and ready. I think that is where the song "Purple Haze" came from. Think about it; the band guys were all sitting on a porch, trying to think of a song that would make them famous. There they sat as the purple haze floated over the neighborhood from all the burning barrels. The head guy started playing. They asked him what he was playing, and he said, "Purple Haze." Yes, sir, I think that's how it might have happened. Anyway, back to the bomb. We saw that Larry's dad had a fire going in his burning barrel, and he went to the garage for some reason. We wandered over and dumped the bomb in the barrel and walked away back to my place. We sat there, and all of a sudden, *Kaboom*. We ran over to Larry's place. His dad was still shaking his head and going "Huh." We looked at the burning barrel. It had a hole about the size of a basketball in the side of it. But we didn't have much time to look at it because we had a lot of spot fires to put out. Larry's dad got his hearing back in a couple of minutes and wanted to know what the two of us had done to his burning barrel. Now Larry never was good in a pressure situation like this, so I took over. I got my best innocent look going, and I said to Larry's dad, "You must have put a spray can in without knowing it." Larry's dad hit himself on the forehead and said, "How could I be that dumb?" I said, "Aw, don't feel bad. It could happen to any one of us." I don't know if he heard me or not because he walked off, shaking his head and kind of mumbling.

DROP AND FALL

I REMEMBER ONE time in eighth-grade woodshop when the teacher was out of the shop. So my great climbing ability came into question. I tried to tell the guys what a great climber I was. But there is always a skeptic or two in every crowd. Our woodshop was about twelve feet high with twelve-inch-wide I beam rafters. My buddy Ted said to these guys, "My pal, Mel, can go up and climb hand over hand on that rafter all the way across the shop." Leave it to my good friend Ted to get me into a tight spot. So I said, "Heck yeah, I could do that, no problem, if I wanted to." These guys said, "There is no way you can do that."

"Yes, he can," Ted said to them. Well, I couldn't let Ted down, and I sure couldn't chicken out, so up I went. I got both hands on the beam, and off I went hand over hand. I got halfway across the shop when the teacher came through the door. He looked and saw me hanging there and said, "Brown, get down from there." So I let go, and down I came. Now, twelve feet is not so far unless you're hanging above a cement floor. Well, I landed light as a cat, but I did not think my feet were going to get me all the way to the principal's office. After the principal and the woodshop teacher got done telling me how badly I could have been hurt, the principal bent me over and hacked my butt. I will tell you that my feet didn't hurt near as much as my behind.

EIGHTH-GRADE TRIP

FINALLY, I WAS coming to the end of my great grade school education. We were going on our outing to Natatorium Park. We called it Nat Park for short. The park started on July 18, 1889. The park ran for seventy-eight years. It closed in 1967. My mother was born in 1902, and she rode the merry-go-round when she was a young child. That same merry-go-round still runs at Riverfront Park in Spokane, Washington. I had a girlfriend at that time. Her name was Shirley. Shirley and I got on the school bus together. We even sat in the same seat. Awe, love was grand. When we got to Nat Park, I bought Shirley a hot dog and some cotton candy. Nothing was too good for my lady. We rode the merry-go-round and the roller coaster. I was saving the tunnel of love for the very last. Shirley saw the octopus and said, "I had always wanted to go on it. Can we, please?" Well, we rode the octopus, and she loved it, and she said, "Let's go again." So off we went again, then she wanted to go again. I said, "OK, but we still have the tunnel of love to go on." Shirley said, "I know, and we will after this, OK?" Off we went on the octopus for the fourth time. We were swinging around and around. All of a sudden, Shirley got a funny look on her face. As we spun around again, she threw up on me and her and anyone else close by. Just like that, the date was over. We never made it to the tunnel of love. Shirley moved away right after graduation. That's when I found out how tough true love can be. I was devastated, but Judy—or was it Susan or was it Jane that smiled at me—I don't know, but I knew that I was over my shattered love affair with Shirley.

GRADUATION

I T WAS NOW graduation time. Loran and I had been picked to do a skit before the diplomas were handed out. I figured that I had better do the skit, or I might not end up with a diploma, so I said "OK" when our teacher asked me to do it. The *Jackie Gleason Show* was big at the time. It was about two guys that were buddies that were always in hot water over some harebrained scheme. I guess they thought Loran and I were qualified to play these parts. I don't know why they would have an idea like that. Anyway, on graduation, we had a table on the stage, and Loran was playing the part of Jackie Gleason, and of course, that made me Art Carney. I only remember one joke that we did. It went like this: I was sitting there, and I started scratching, and Loran said, "Why are you scratching?" I said, "Because no one else knows where I itch." Oh, the crowd went wild with that one. Well, maybe not wild, but they did laugh. And just like that, I was ready for high school. I guess the question was, "Is high school ready for me?"

Mels 8th grade Graduation.

SUMMERTIME AGAIN

I WAS OUT of school and back on the farm for the summer, and it's haying time. My uncle Boyd said to me, "You want to run the tractor and the mower?" Heck yes, I always wanted to run the tractor, and they let me because they knew how good I was. But as I think back, that might not have been the real reason they let me mow. I would be mowing along, and I would mow over a yellow jackets nest. Now here in northern Idaho, yellow jacket sometimes build their nest on the ground or at the base of a tree just as you're tying the cowboy up. So you mow over a ground nest that you never see, and all of a sudden, you get stung right in the back of the head. Now you have to get the tractor stopped and jump and run. If you're lucky, you only get stung eight or more times before you get out of range. You then have to wait until dark and sneak down with a can of bug spray to where the tractor and mower are parked. You spray those suckers and get the heck of out there. In the morning, those yellow jackets are graveyard dead. You then go back to mowing and hope there are no more nests in the field. When I got all done mowing for the year, I had only run over five or six nests. Take that times eight, and you can figure out what my head looked like by the end of the season. I said to myself that it was the last year I was going to run the tractor and mower because I wasn't going through that misery every summer. The next summer rolled around, and Uncle Boyd said, "You want to run the tractor and mower this year?" I said, "Heck yes, because after all, I am the best tractor driver and hay mower in northern Idaho or maybe all of Idaho."

Hay field on the farm

Mel on tractor, grandma Lewis
standing on top of the hay

Mel driving and hauling hay

RAT HUNTING

WELL, ONE SUMMER, Dad told me that there was a pack rat in the barn, and he was packing stuff from all over the farm and stashing it up in the rafters of the barn. He even got into Grandma's root cellar and started packing her carrots off to the barn, and if Grandma wasn't happy, there wasn't anyone who was going to be happy. So Dad called on me because he knew that I was the best rat hunter in northern Idaho and maybe the whole state of Idaho. Dad said, "Get your brother Doran and show him the fine art of rat hunting." Well, that's not exactly what he said. He said, "Make sure you don't take your little brother Doran rat hunting with you. He is too young, and I would like to see him get older." After Dad left, I got to thinking about that, and I thought Doran should learn rat hunting from an expert rat hunter, and that would be me. So I told Doran I was going to take him rat hunting, but I made him promise not to tell Dad. Doran said, "OK." I think maybe I should have gotten a stronger commitment from him than just an "OK." Anyway, we went down to the barn and scouted it out. I was pretty sure where that old pack rat was going to be tonight, so I told Doran, "Let's get ready." We went up to the house, and I got the .12-gauge shotgun and the six-battery flashlight, and we got to the barn just before dark. We settled down. I gave Doran the flashlight and told him, "When I touch you on the arm, you turn on the flashlight and point it at that beam right there." He said, "OK." We sat there about an hour, or maybe it was ten minutes. Time drags on when you're hunting rats. Finally, I heard that pack rat up on the beam, so I gave him a little more time, then nudged Doran's arm. He turned on the flashlight. Jazam, that rat was not where I thought he should have been. He was on a beam about six feet from us. Well, I aimed the .12 gauge and pulled the trigger. *Boom.* It was a little loud in there. After the smoke cleared and Doran picked the flashlight up, we shined it up where the rat had been. There was an eight-inch hole in the barn wall. All that was left of the rat was his nose and the end of his tail. I thought that Dad would not care for the eight-inch hole in the barn wall because he had told me not to use the .12

gauge. He thought that my .22 rifle would have been just fine to use. But dang, I loved that .12 gauge. My shoulder not so much, but when you have big rats to kill, there's nothing like the .12 gauge. Well, I had Doran sworn to secrecy, and I figured that I could fix the hole in the wall before Dad saw it and I was home free. We walked up to the house, and Doran went in ahead of me and said, "We got that big sucker." Dad said, "I assume that that 'big sucker' means the pack rat?" Before I could jump in and halt this travesty that was about to befall me, Doran said, "Yeah, Mel took that big old .12 gauge and blew a big hole in the wall, and all that was left of the rat was the tip of his nose and the tip of his tail." Dad looked at me and said, "I assume that your little brother was with you tonight in the barn?" Before I could come up with a good answer, Doran said, "Yeah, it was great. I learned all about rat hunting." Then he said, "But I don't think I'm big enough for that .12 gauge yet, but I think I could sure use the .410-gauge shotgun for sure." Dad said, "You are not big enough for the .410 either." Doran said, "Well, I ain't too small because brother has been letting me shoot ground squirrels with the .410 all summer." Just as I saw the red marks working up Dad's neck and I knew that I was in a heap of big trouble, Mom stepped in and said, "Boys, it is bedtime." Well, you weren't getting any argument from me. I was in bed before the lamp wick quit glowing. I don't know what Mom said to Dad that night, but in the morning, all Dad said as he went out the door was "Have the barn wall fixed by the time I get home." Mom looked at me and said, "Don't ask, just get your butt out to the barn, and get that wall fixed." I thought to myself, *Dang, I beat the grim reaper again. Thanks, Mom.*

This is the old barn where I
shot the pack rat.

RAT IN THE TRUCK

IN HIGH SCHOOL, I worked by unloading produce trucks at night for a big local warehouse. One night, I got a call to come unload a potato truck that was due in at midnight. The boss said, "You will have Jerome and Wes to help you." I thought to myself, *Jerome will be drunk by midnight, so we will just put him in the corner. Wes is too old to lift one-hundred-pound potato sacks, so he will run the forklift. So looks like a long night.* Good thing it was Friday night—no school the next day. I got there just as the truck backed in, and Jerome was just drunk enough that he thought he was Hercules. All right, I was going to put him to work and keep him sober as long as I could. We opened the doors, and the light shined in, and sitting on the potato sacks was one big-assed rat just looking at us. We slammed the doors shut and wondered what to do. Now the warehouse was not in the best part of town. Jerome lived in one of the many flophouses close to the warehouse. He told me once that he paid two dollars and fifty cents a week for rent, and he had a rough time making that. I think his liquid diet had something to do with that. But Jerome said, "I know where we can get the biggest, meanest street cat there is. He ain't ever lost a fight that I know of, and he hangs out down where I live." So off we went to find this cat, which we did, and Jerome picked him up, and we took him back to the warehouse. We opened one door on the truck and threw the cat in and slammed the door shut. We heard the cat screaming, and we just knew that he was kicking ass and taking names. We felt kind of sorry for the rat. Finally, the noise died down, so we opened the door. That cat came screaming out between our legs and down the loading dock, and he was gone. We looked in the truck, and the rat was still sitting on the potato sacks like nothing happened. So we got some potatoes and threw them at the rat. All of a sudden, he jumped down and went out between our legs and down the loading ramp. I guess he wanted some more of that cat.

THE DUMP

I REMEMBER MY brother Gordon and I went on a road trip to the coast. We were staying at my aunt Elaine and uncle Gordy's place. Our cousin Dave came in and said, "You guys want to go rat hunting?" Well, you know the answer to that: heck yes. Dave said, "Good. We're going to meet some of my buddies at the dump after dark. Be ready about eight o'clock." I said, "We did not bring any guns with us." Dave said, "Awe, don't worry about it. We have it covered." We piled into Dave's rig and headed out. We left Smoky Point and headed out toward Lake Goodman. We turned onto Frank Water Road and wound through the countryside until we came to the warm beach dump. We parked our rigs, facing the top edge of the dump. Dave and his buddies jumped out of their rigs and popped their hoods open. They brought out spotlights and hooked them to their car batteries. I asked where the guns were, and they just laughed and said, "Guns? We don't need no stinking guns." With that said, they all pulled baseball bats out and handed Gordon and me each a bat. They then told everyone to shut up, and we did, and what we heard coming up the face of the dump were thousands of *rats*. All of a sudden, the guys turned on the spotlights, and there were rats right at our feet. Now I am a great rat hunter, but I have never seen that many rats in one place in my life. I kind of started wondering how tight my pant cuffs were. Well, we started whaling away with our baseball bats, and there were rats flying every which way. Dave and I saw this mattress lying on the ground, so we went over to see what might be under it. Well, Gordy was standing in front of the mattress. I reached down and grabbed the mattress and picked it up. Under it was the biggest rat any of us had ever seen. Well, cousin Dave reared back and whacked that rat with all he had. That rat flew up and hit my brother Gordy right in the chest and kind of hung there forever. Well, he turned white and started to back up, but his legs weren't working right. All he did was kind of stand in midair with his legs flailing and that dead rat just hanging on.

Finally, his legs hit the ground, and he backed up, and the rat fell to the ground, and he was safe. Now, all the guys found this to be the funniest thing they had ever seen, including me. Little brother not so much. He thought that we were barbarians. He finally did see the humor in it about twenty years later.

MUMBLY-PEG

ANOTHER GREAT GAME we played was called Mumbly-peg. This was back when boys could bring their pocket knives to school, and guess what? No one got stabbed—well, not on purpose anyway. Oh, I forgot. You want to know how to play Mumbly peg. Well, you play it with a knife and a Mumbly peg. First off, you get another guy that wants to play, and that's not hard because all the boys wanted to play Mumbly peg. OK, you cut a twig about the size of a matchstick. You sharpen one end, and then you start it into ground. Each guy that is playing gets to hit the peg three times with his knife handle. This usually drives the peg down to ground level or below ground level. If this happens, the guys shout, "Root, root." I will explain this a little later. The guys would pick who would start playing, which was usually the guy that got everyone together to play. He would take his knife, grab it by the blade, and flip it once and stick it in the ground. Then the second guy had to do the same thing. If he did, you went on to round two. The second guy would then go first. He would put the point of his knife on the back of his right hand and flip it, and if it stuck in the ground, the first guy then had to do the same thing. If he made it, we went to the third round. It went like this until someone missed. Whoever missed was declared the loser and had to root the Mumbly peg. This is how you had to do it: You put your hands behind your back and got down on your knees. You bend over and put your head to the ground. You then had to get a hold of the peg with your teeth and pull it out of the ground. This is where the name Mumbly peg comes from because as you root the peg from the ground, you mumble a lot as you try to strain the dirt and sod out of your teeth as you go for the peg. As I told you early on, I was the best knife thrower in northern Idaho or maybe the whole state of Idaho. That's why I could never figure out why I had to root the peg out so many times.

THE FLYTRAP

MY GRANDFATHER WAS very talented. If he had a need for something, he would just make it. I saw him make his own band saw. He built his own water pressure system without using a pump. He had no electricity to run a pump. So he went up on the mountain and dug out his spring. He then built a one-thousand-gallon concrete holding tank. When the tank was full, the overflow then filled our pond in the front yard. That is the pond I told you about where we put the trout we caught in the creek. From the holding tank, he ran a three-inch pipe and reduced that down to a one-inch pipe into the house. This gave them thirty pounds of pressure at the house. We were able to water our garden and yard all without electricity. In the summertime, we had lots of flies and yellow jackets. My grandpa thought about this and put his skills to work and built the trap. The trap was built with four wooden legs, a solid top, and a solid bottom that had a six-inch hole in it. The bottom was raised about four inches from ground level. Grandpa then took a window screen and made a funnel six inches wide at the bottom. The funnel was about twelve inches tall and with a very tiny hole at the top. He then attached the funnel over the hole in the bottom, facing up toward the top board. He then wrapped the outside with a window screen so that the funnel was totally enclosed. Here is how it worked: I would go down to the lake and catch some perch and then put them under the trap. The flies would smell the fish and fly in to eat. When a fly takes off, it always goes straight up. As it does, it flies up into the funnel. It goes up to the top of the funnel. It crawls through the tiny hole, and it is trapped. By the end of summer, our traps were all full of dead flies. Thinking about the flytraps brings a memory of my grandpa and his sense of humor. Grandpa and I were down at the general store, talking to old Bill, when a man and woman came in from somewhere. It took us about two seconds to figure out that they weren't from around here. The woman started talking to my grandfather. She asked, "Do you have electricity?" Grandpa said, "No, we don't, but I do have a great flytrap." She said, "That's nice." Grandpa said,

"Yes, it is. I caught over ten thousand flies this year. I think that might be a record for these parts." She said, "You mean you counted all of those flies? Why?" Grandpa, with a straight face, said, "Well, we're real poor around here, so we have to help ourselves and each other out." She said, "But why do you have to count flies? How will that help you or the others around here?" Grandpa, straight-faced and all, looked at her and said, "Well, us being so poor, we take the flies and knock the wings off, and we eat them like raisins all winter. The reason I count them is that my wife and I can only eat about eight thousand flies ourselves for the winter, so we share the other two thousand with our neighbors. We also sell a few of them. I think Bill here might have a package or two if you would like to buy some." The lady shuddered, grabbed her husband, and said, "Come on, let's get out of here before it gets dark." And I said, "That's a good idea because the Sanctamoojas come out after dark." And just like that, they were gone. We laughed our heads off about the fly part. But I was plum serious about the Sanctamooja part.

MIGHTY FINE PORCUPINE

TED AND I were up on the cliff above our upper hay field. We were looking into the trees just below the cliff. We saw a porcupine high up in a tree, so we decided to shoot it, and we did. It crashed down through the tree and landed on the ground at the base of the tree. We had to walk about a quarter of a mile to get down the cliff area to get down to the porcupine. I said to Ted, "Dang, he's a big one. Maybe we ought to eat him?" Ted said, "Yeah, I always wanted to eat me a big old porcupine." So we went down to the barn and got a five-gallon bucket. We walked back up to where the porky was laying and stuffed him in the bucket—carefully, I might add. Grab the wrong place on a porcupine, and you aren't going to like it. Those quills are sharp little buggers. You haven't lived until you have extracted porcupine quills from you or other animals. I will talk about that later. We took the porky down to the house. Grandma was in the kitchen. I told Grandma that we had a nice big porcupine and we were thinking about eating it. Grandma said, "You boys skin it, and I'll cook it for you." Well, all right. Ted and I were wondering how to skin this thing when Uncle Boyd came along. He said, "Boys, you got yourselves a good old big one there. What are you going to do with it?" Well, I told Uncle Boyd, "We've been thinking we would eat it if we can figure out how to skin it." Uncle Boyd said, "Shoot, that ain't hard. You just roll him over on his back. His belly is soft, and it has no quills. Open him up, and skin him just like that." We did it just like Uncle Boyd said to, then we hung him up and let him cool overnight. Grandma started cooking old porky about one o'clock in the afternoon, and by dinnertime, it's ready to eat. She put it on the table, and Ted and I looked at it and wondered if we should eat it or not. Grandpa and Boyd both said, "Let's eat this thing," and they both dived in and cut off big old chunks of meat and started eating. So Ted and I got some meat, and with great misgivings, we took a taste, and dang, it tasted just like greasy old pork. Grandma had cooked it with potatoes and carrots. It was some good eating, and I ain't lying. I found out later on that Grandma and Grandpa and Uncle Boyd had been funning Ted and me because they had been brought up eating porcupine. I was a little surprised that Grandpa had not tried to throw in some fly raisins for dessert.

QUILLS

I TOLD YOU that I had some porcupine-quill stories to tell, so here they are. We had an old dog named Dudley. He was half a German shepherd and half of something else. Now, old Dudley was very intelligent except when it came to porcupines. He was just plum stupid. If we let him out at night, he would come home in the morning with a face full of quills. Then we would have to hold Dudley down and start removing quills. Now, most people don't know how to remove quills. They just try to pull the quills out with pliers, which is very painful for the dog. If you don't get the quills out, they keep working their way into the dog because the quills have little barbs on the outside that keep the quill going into the dog. The barbs will not let the quill come back out. The reason the barbs work is because the quill is full of air. All you have to do is take a pair of side dikes and cut the quill in half. This lets the air out of the quill. It then collapses. Thus the barbs lose their bite, and the quill can be pulled with ease. Of course, Dudley doesn't know all of this, so he just wants to tear your arm off while you're trying to help him. That's why you'll need all the help you can get just to hold him down. Well, you get all the quills out of Dudley, and he is OK. But don't let him out after dark, or in the morning, you will get do it all over again. Dudley just could not resist a good porcupine fight; the fact that he lost every time did not seem to register with him.

PORCUPINE PATROL

I REMEMBER ONE time Doran and I got a porcupine trapped under the barn. We took a one-by-four board and stuck it in where the porky was, and *whack*, he slapped it with his tail and drove his quills all the way through the board. Moral of the story is if you are going to mess with a porcupine, don't do it from behind. Doran and I were on porcupine patrol one night. What's that? You want to know what porcupine patrol is? Well, in the late spring when the apple trees are starting to grow new buds, that's when the porcupines love to climb the trees and eat the new buds. When this happens, you don't get any apples, and that means no cider or apple sauce for the winter. We can't have that. So we kids would patrol the apple trees, and we would try to scare the porkies out of the trees. If that didn't work, then we would have to shoot one of them. That usually scared them off. Then we would leave the dead one at the base of the tree. That would keep them from coming back. Doran and I went down into the meadow about ten o'clock at night. We had two big old apple trees down there. We snuck up to the tree, and Doran turned the flashlight on, and dang, if there weren't five porkies up in the tree. We started hollering and shaking the tree. But they just looked at us and kept right on eating the new buds. Doran was standing under the tree with the light shining up into it. I had my .22 rifle with me, so I aimed and shot and hit a big old porky. Down he came, bouncing off the limbs on the way down. We could hear him coming. Doran lost him with the light. Anyway, down he came and landed right at Doran's feet. Another foot and Doran would be wearing the sucker—not good. Well, in the morning, we pulled some of the quills to add to our collection of ground squirrel tails and pheasant feathers. I think that my horse Buck beat us to the quills because he came walking up to us, and he had five quills sticking out of his nose. Knowing Buck's temperament, I figured this was going to be fun. Well, we led Buck up to the barn, and I got the clippers and pliers out and went to work. I was ready to get my brains kicked out, but old Buck just stood there and let me take those quills out of his nose. When I got done with that, I turned him loose. As if to say thank you, Buck jumped in the air, farted, and ran around the barnyard.

MELVIN BROWN

WINGS IN THE NIGHT

I MENTIONED OUR great collection of ground squirrel tails. You see, as long as we were hunting ground squirrels, Grandpa would buy our ammunition. You see, ground squirrels are the scourge of hay fields because they dig their burrows and leave big mounds of dirt. And that was very hard on our haying equipment. So when we shot them, we would cut their tails off and show them to Grandpa. When we had fifty tails, we got another box of .22 shells. I also had a .22 special with an octagon barrel. This would only mean something to you gun nuts out there. The .22 special had a longer casing than a regular .22 long rifle. Thereby, it had more power than a regular .22. But the bullets cost more, so we used it sparingly. The main use of the .22 special was the fact that you could bring down deer if you hit them just right. But the main thing was you could bring down a deer with very little noise, which was quite important in certain hunting situations. Ground squirrels were smart little critters. You could not hunt in only one place because they would get wise quickly and not come into the open. So we great white hunters had to roam far and wide to get our quota of squirrel tails. I want to talk to you about something that used to spook my brothers and me. You see, we had to change irrigation pipes at all different times of the day or night. Now we had Chinese ringneck pheasants all over our country, and they loved to hang out in our alfalfa fields. Any of you that have been around pheasants know what kind of sound they make when they take off. So my brothers and I were out at midnight in the alfalfa, changing irrigation pipes. Now these birds sleep in the hay fields at night because it was easy for them to hide out. So we were out there at midnight, which is spooky enough. But when you almost step on a pheasant, that sucker blasts straight up into the air and lets out these strange sounds as it flies away. One good thing though: you could pee your pants from fright, and no one would know it because your pants were already wet from changing irrigation pipes. Our most fun thing to do was to invite a friend from the city to stay overnight and take him out to change pipes in the middle of the night. We would let the guest be the guy out on the front end of the pipe so he could experience the great feeling of hearing the wings in the night.

Mel hunting ground squirrels   Mel hunting

THE BUNNY HOP

I AM SURE you have heard about the one-room schoolhouse. Well, we really did have one. It sat up on the hill right above the local sawmill. The sawmill was owned and run by Jim and his three sons. All the ranchers and farmers would cut logs and haul them down to the mill to have lumber made or to sell to help meet their expenses. But come Saturday night, it was time for the dance. Everyone from miles around came to the dance. People would come and bring things to eat and drink. They would bring the kids and turn 'em loose. The school had a hardwood floor that they would sprinkle with fine sawdust to make the floor slippery so it was easier to dance on. They needed it to be easy because they danced all night nonstop. Everyone would waltz and square dance and do the bunny hop. You want to know what the bunny hop is? Well, everyone gets in a line. As soon as you hear the bunny hop music, run to the dance floor. Find a place in line. Place your hands on the hips of the person in front of you. Allow the person behind you to grab your hips as well. Following the song lyrics, kick your right foot out to the side, placing your heel on the ground. Bring your right foot back in. Then do the same thing again, kicking your right foot out to the side. Bring it back in again. Kick your left foot out to the side, placing your heel on the ground. Bring your left foot back in. Then you do it again, kicking your left foot out to the side. Bring it back in. Hop forward once with both feet together. Hop backward once with both feet together. Hop forward three times with the music. Repeat the steps, holding on to the person in front of you until the music stops. Now when the bunny hop music started, us boys would run out the door and go down under the schoolhouse. The schoolhouse was built on the side of the hill, so it was eight feet from the floor to the ground. Because we had George and Lena, they were the official bunny hop leaders. They had a ranch close by, and they never missed the dance. George was not a big man, but you could tell that he worked hard every day. He was all muscle. Now we come to Lena. Let us say that Lena ate well. We asked George how it was dancing with Lena, and George said, "It's great. All I have to do is hang on." Well, as I said, George and Lena were the bunny hop leaders, so we kids were under the schoolhouse floor. We could always tell where the head of the line was. We could see the floor move whenever George and Lena hopped forward three times. Meanwhile, out in the parking lot, there would be teenage boys strutting their stuff and fighting now and then. I remember one night when I was dancing with a cute little filly and enjoying myself profusely. Well, I took a little break and went outside for some fresh air when this big redneck kid came up to me and started telling me what he was going to do to me if I danced with his girl one more time. I said, "What girl? Oh, you mean sweet little Melisa? Yeah, I like dancing with her." Now this was probably farther than I should have gone with this stupid big kid because he had a reputation for annihilating little young punks like me, but I could not help myself. Well, just about the time I was about to lose my life, everyone heard my little brother Doran. He was standing on the porch railing, right behind this big ape, with a jack handle in his hand. He hollered at the big guy, "You leave my big brother alone, or I am going to cave your head in." The big guy looked at Doran, whom he could have swatted like a bug, and started laughing. We all laughed and went back to the dance. Melisa and I were over at least for the rest of that night. The old guys went back to talking about tractors and farming. These are memories that I would not have missed for anything.

THE HAMMER DRAW

I WAS DOWNSTAIRS one day, working on my model railroad, which, I might add, had claimed most of the basement. Oh, it was a great layout. It had about three hundred feet of track laid down. It had a town built on it, and all the buildings had lights in them, and it had a town square. One of the best features was the Harry's Hangout, which was patterned after the 1950-style drive-in. Oh, it was cool. I had a lake and farms and tunnels—all the neat stuff. All the kids in the neighborhood would come over and help with the trains and building stuff. Well, this particular morning, I was working alone when Darryl snuck up on me and hollered, "Draw." I turned around with a hammer in my hand and drew. Just as Darryl was clearing leather, my hammer came up, but I did not have a good grip for drawing my hammer. It flew from my hand and hit Darryl in the mouth, thereby chipping his front tooth—not good. I told Darryl, "I'm sorry about your tooth, but you can't go sneaking up on a great gunslinger like me and hollering 'draw.'" Darryl mumbled that it made sense to him but not so much to his parents or mine. By the time they had Darryl's tooth fixed, they told us that there would be no more hammer drawing. We sort of heard them. But it did not register with us because we were too busy making wooden swords.

THE DRAIN

WELL, WE WERE over at the pool, swimming and having a great time. This made me think of one of the cute things that we would do. We were all great swimmers, and underwater, none were finer than our gang. What we would do was pick one of the guys to be it. He would have to dive down to the bottom at the ten-foot end of the pool. The pool drains were in the ten-foot end of the pool. They had big iron grates over the drain handle. But if your hand and arm were small enough, you could reach through the grate and turn the drain handle. We would do this because we were stupid at the time, and it was fun to open the drains and see how long it took for the lifeguard to see that the pool water was going down. He would then have to get his long turn on handle to reach down and turn the valve closed. So one day, we were at the pool, and we thought that it's time to pull the drain trick again. We could only do this great trick about three times in a summer to keep the lifeguard from catching us. We picked Larry to go down, so down he went. We're watching Larry. He got down to the drain, and he stayed down there, and we were all saying, "Dang, we didn't know that Larry could stay underwater that long. He must have a set of lungs bigger than all of us together." We kept watching Larry down there. All of a sudden, the lifeguard jumped in and went down to where Larry's hand was caught in the drain grate. He got Larry's hand loose, brought him up, and went to work on him. Finally, Larry coughed and started breathing again, and they hauled him off to the hospital. They kicked us out of the pool for a week. And our great drain trick did not happen again that I know of. I know that good old Larry never went near the drains again, but he did want to know which one of us brave guys pulled him up out of the pool. I told him, "Awe, we don't want to talk about it. We just did what we had to do."

MULE AND THE YELLOW JACKETS

BEING THAT I had a week off from the pool, old DW and I thought it was a good time to do some mule logging. Grandpa needed a bunch of fence posts, so we took our mule old Jack, and off we went to the back forty. We had our trusty Homelite chain saw with us. It was one of the early saws on the market. All I can say about the lite part is that it was a slight exaggeration by about ten pounds, but it was about ten pounds lighter than our old McCulloch chain saw. You had to mix your oil and gas at a forty-to-one mix so that when you hit the throttle, you had a big blue cloud surrounding you. One thing about it: the yellow jackets would not come in to the blue cloud after you. We picked out and cut the logs we wanted and hooked the mule to a log and started pulling when all of a sudden, the mule started going nuts. He jumped off the trail, and the log got hung up, and he couldn't move, then we saw what was wrong with him. We had run over a yellow jacket nest. DW had the Homelite in his hands. He fired it up and hit the throttle, and the blue cloud protected us. But old Jack, the mule, was still going bonkers, and then we saw why. The yellow jackets were in old Jack's ear, stinging him badly. DW ran over and put the saw up by Jack's ear and hit the throttle. The blue cloud drove the yellow jackets away. I got old Jack unhooked, and we got away. I only got stung twice while unhooking the mule—not bad. We did have one problem after that. When DW used the chain saw to save old Jack, he had the muffler pointed right into the mule's left ear. So for about six months, we had to come up to old Jack on the right side where he could hear you, or you would scare him, and he would try to kick your brains out. Now, there are some people that would say it would only take one kick for me.

THE WASP NEST

I WAS WALKING past the barn one day when I saw this gigantic wasp nest hanging from the eaves of the barn. You ask me what the difference is between a yellow jacket and a wasp. There's a big difference. A yellow jacket, as the name infers, is yellow with black stripes and is about half the size of a wasp. The wasp is black and white. There is a big difference: there tends to be more yellow jackets around, so you hear more about them. A yellow jacket is a mean mohumer and will sting you just for the heck of it. But it can only sting you once because it leaves its stinger and half of its butt stuck in your arm or, in my case, head and neck. Now here is the big difference: a wasp can sting you more than once. He is not as mean as a yellow jacket, but when you get him mad, he can put a world of hurt on you. A yellow jacket is not smart but just mean because when he stings you just for the heck of it, he is signing his own death warrant. Not so with a wasp; he just keeps on giving and giving. So as I was saying, I spied this big wasp nest hanging from the barn. I found my uncle Boyd and told him about the nest. We went down to the barn to check it out. Uncle Boyd said, "Boy howdy, that is a big sucker." He then said, "Meet me down here after dark tonight, and I will show you how to take care of this wasp nest." Now, I was a little apprehensive about what Uncle Boyd had in store for me. It got dark, and I went down to the barn. Uncle Boyd was there, and he had a ladder with him. I already didn't like the looks of this. Uncle Boyd said to me, "I want you to carefully put this ladder up the wall until you get it up under the wasp nest." Now this ladder was not one of the new aluminum ladders that they have nowadays. No, this was a homemade ladder. It was made of two poles, about twenty feet long and about four inches in diameter at the bottom. About every sixteen inches, there was a rough cut, one by four, nailed to the poles to form the rungs of the ladder. I don't think this ladder weighed more than a hundred pounds. Uncle Boyd said to me, "Now, be sure you don't make any noise when you put the ladder up. You don't want to wake those suckers up." I finally got the ladder in place without waking the wasps up. Uncle Boyd then handed me a paper shopping bag and said to me, "OK, climb up the ladder and carefully put the bag over the wasp nest, then knock the nest off into the bag and make sure you hold the bag closed." I looked at my uncle and asked him, "Why don't you do this?" He said to me, "No, you need to learn how to do this. After all, I am teaching you something that most people don't know about." I said, "I am not sure that most people want to know about this." Boyd said to me, "What's the matter? Are you a little sissy boy now? Are you afraid to do something great like this?" Now that right there was not fair as I always wanted to do something great, so I said, "OK." I slowly climbed up the ladder. When I got up under the nest, I could hear some strange noises inside the nest. I slowly slipped the bag over the nest and whacked the nest off into the bag. Then that bag came alive. I was afraid that it was going to fly off and take me with it. I could hear a million wasps inside that bag. I was now looking to see if there were any holes in that bag. I should have done that before I went up the ladder. Well, I came down that ladder, holding that bag closed with a death grip. When I got down, Uncle Boyd had a small fire going in the middle of the lane. He had some twine, and he tied the top of the bag shut. Now, as we listened to this bag, I asked Boyd, "Are you sure the fire will kill all of them?" Boyd said, "Sure. No problem. Just to show you how sure I am, I'm going to let you throw the bag in the fire. I will be standing way over here just to make sure you do it right." I said, "OK. I am glad you are looking out for me, but maybe you should be a little closer to make sure I do it right." Boyd said, "No, because my far eyesight is better than my short eyesight." Well, that made sense to me, so I threw the bag in the fire. Now, I can report that Uncle Boyd's fire theory was about 95 percent accurate. When that bag got a hole burned in it, about 5 percent of those wasps got out alive, and they were not happy. Now, 5 percent does not sound like much, but if you take 5 percent of a million wasps, that's a bunch. Like I said, those wasps were not happy, so I and my dog Duffus took off. I ran down toward the creek, and I jumped down in the tall grass. The wasps didn't see me. Whew. All of a sudden, Duffus ran in a big circle with the wasps after him. He ran over and plopped down beside me. Here came the wasps. *Whap.* I got stung. I jumped up, and into the creek I went. Duffus went running off with the wasps right on his butt. He didn't come home until morning. When I finally made my way to the house, soaking wet, Uncle Boyd was sitting at the kitchen table, eating an apple pie. He said to me, "Wasn't killing all those wasps enough? You had to go swimming in the middle of the night too?" I said, "Uncle Boyd, I don't have time to talk. I have to go take care of all these wasp stings in the back of my head." He said, "You know, for a young lad, you sure seem to get stung a lot."

This is the ladder I mention in
the wasp nest story.

MELVIN BROWN

THE SNIPE HUNT

OUR BOY SCOUT troop went on a wintertime campout. The church that sponsored our troop had a church camp out on the Spokane River near Post Falls, Idaho. There was a cement block cookhouse and a big dock on the river and lots of places for us to pitch our tents. Now, we had about ten new tenderfoot scouts with us. For those of you that don't know what a tenderfoot scout is, let me explain. A tenderfoot scout is a boy that is just starting in the Boy Scouts, so you know that we older scouts just have to lead these poor, unsuspecting boys down the right path. Yep. So for a couple of weeks before the big campout, we started telling the tenderfoot scouts about the great time we have in store for them. There will be hikes, camp-cooking lessons, lessons on how to set up your tents and campsites, and last but not least, a giant snipe hunt. Oh, they were so excited, but they asked, "What is a snipe?" Well, I told them, "It is a little black bird that is a cross between a roadrunner and a hummingbird." They said, "How can that be?" I told them, "They are fast on the ground, but they can stop on a dime and hover. That's why you have to catch them while they are still on the ground and running. If they start flying, you will not catch them." The tenderfoot scouts asked, "How do we catch them then?" I told them, "All will be revealed after we get camp set up." We got to the campsite and got all set up. It takes most of the day to get everything done. The tension was so high that we had a hard time holding the tenderfeet's attention. All day they were ready for the snipe hunt. Just before dark, we called them all together, and I started to explain how the snipe hunt would be done. We passed out gunnysacks to all the tenderfeet, and right away, they wanted to know what the sacks were for. I told them, "This is what you are going to catch the snipe in." Joey said, "How are we going to catch the snipe in this gunnysack when they run as fast as you say they do?"

"Joey, Joey, you question our knowledge on snipe hunting. I am shocked that no one told you that we hold the state championship for snipe hunting." Joey said, "Well then, how do we do it?" "Well, first off, you need to go out before it gets dark and cut a willow stick that you can bend into a U shape. That will hold your bag open." Out they went hunting for just the right stick. Jim said to me, "You think these guys are dumb enough to believe all of this?" I said, "Jim, trust me. I know dumb when I see it." All the tenderfeet came back in with their sticks, and they placed them in their sacks. I said, "Boys, those are some of the best-looking snipe sacks I have ever seen." Joey said, "You told us that snipes are black, so how are we supposed to see them in the dark?"

"I am glad you asked that question, Joey. This is why you have us experienced snipe hunters guiding you. You see, Joey, this is why we only hunt snipe in the wintertime because there is snow on the ground, and, Joey, what color is snow?" And just like that, a light went off in Joey's brain, and he said, "White. Snow is white, and snipes are black." Then Joey asked, "But how do we get the snipe to run into our bags?" I thought to myself, *this is just too easy.* This might be why I went just a little bit overboard. I said, "Joey, we are going to put you guys in the center of the best snipe-hunting clearing in the state of Idaho. We will place you guys back-to-back in a circle in the middle of the clearing, and then, we will go out to the edge of the clearing and make loud noises to drive the snipes to you." Joey asked, "You said that they can fly if they need to. What can we do to stop that from happening?"

"I am glad you asked that. This is why I am passing out these shiny pie pans. I want you to tie these pie pans onto your hats." Joey said, "What good is that going to do?"

"Glad you asked that, Joey. Dang, you are one sharp cookie. I can't put nothing over on you. OK, here is what you will see. You'll see the snipes coming because they are black and the snow is white. When the snipe gets close to your bag, he will fly, and you will miss him, but there is one thing that will keep him from flying. You see, snipes will not fly in the daylight, so all you have to do is shine your flashlight up onto your pie pan. This will reflect the light down to the ground, and this will cause the snipe to run right into your sack." Now, I knew that was pushing it, but it was so funny, I could not help it, and I knew that when the tenderfeet found out how stupid they were, they would laugh just as much as we did, maybe. Off we went. We took them to a clearing that we knew about that was up a steep hill and about one mile from camp. We got them back-to-back in the middle of the clearing with their bags open and ready. I told them that we would go out into the trees and start making noises and driving the snipes into them. We got into the woods and started beating on our mess kits and hollering and backing up into the woods. We then left and went back to camp, leaving the tenderfoot scouts sitting in the middle of the clearing, waiting for the snipes to come out. We went to our tents and went to bed, thinking that the tenderfeet would soon come struggling into camp. About midnight, our scoutmaster went from tent to tent, waking us all up, and he told us to get to the cook shack. We got into the shack. I can tell right away that the scoutmaster was not too happy with us. He said to us, "What did you guys do to the tenderfoot scouts?" Well, of course, they let me do the talking. I said, "Uh . . . uh . . . uh . . . uh . . . uh . . . well, we sort of took them snipe hunting and left them up in the clearing. We thought that they would be back by now." But the scoutmaster said, "Well, they're not back, and I suggest you people get out there and find them now, and they had better be all right. Do you understand?" We did understand, and out the door we went. When we got to the clearing, there was no one there—not good. The guys all asked me what happened to those tenderfeet. I said, "I don't know, but we better start looking for them." Well, we looked up and down the river in all the clearings. We knew of no scouts. We hunted for them until first light. We then decided that they must have all drowned in the river and that we must go back to camp and face the music. As we drew closer to camp, we saw smoke rising from the cook shack. We were all cold and wet, but we still did not want to go into the cook shack and face Bud, but we did. I pushed the door open, and what I saw inside were all the tenderfoot scouts sitting at tables, eating bacon, eggs, and hotcakes and laughing their heads off. We then found out what had happened. Joey stood up and told us, "The scoutmaster had come up to the clearing after you had abandoned us and hid all of us until he woke all of you up to go look for us. Then we slept in the cook shack nice and warm while you were out freezing your butts, looking for us." I thought to myself, *I knew that Joey the tenderfoot was going to be trouble. He thinks too much.* But what really chapped my butt was what Joey said to me. He said, "We knew that when you older scouts found out how stupid you were that you would laugh just as much as we did."

CAT STORIES

LIKE I SAID, back then we always had a ton of cats around the place, so I am going to tell you a couple of cat stories. Well, our mama cat Patches was about to have kittens any day. One morning, we saw Patches, and we could tell that she had had her kittens, but we couldn't find them anywhere. Patches was meowing and pacing around, and then she took off, running into the shop building. We followed her into the shop. Now, we could hear the kittens, but we couldn't find them. Then we saw Patches jump up on top of the tractor and then jump up through the crawl space and into the attic. We got a ladder and went up into the attic. There were two kittens there, so we knew that Patches had them there. So after looking around, we figured out what had happened. The shop wall had no insulation and was open at the top, so we knew that some of the kittens had fallen into the wall. We went down into the shop and started listening with our ears up against the wall. We finally figured out which wall cavity they were in. So we grabbed the saber saw and cut a hole about two feet up the wall, hoping that the kittens would be below the cut. They were, and we fished out four sawdust-covered kittens. We built a nice bed for them and Patches in a dark corner of the shop, and they all made it OK.

BLACK CAT

OUR BIG OLD black mama cat had a litter of kittens out in the barn. There were six kittens. One male was jet-black, and I liked him a lot. Well, the kittens were about three weeks old when we went out to the barn, and we found the little black kitten had a grain sack fall on him, and he had a broken front leg. We called the vet, and he told us there was nothing we could do for him and that we would have to put him down. Well, Doran and I just said, "Awe, what the heck does he know anyway?" So we took the little black cat, and we went to work on him. We took two Popsicle sticks and a roll of adhesive tape. We built a heavy-duty splint for the little guy. We turned him back in with his brothers and sister and hoped for the best. Well, little black cat found out that he could use that cast in a way that we would never have guessed. The cast turned into the best weapon he could ask for. When it came around to feeding time, he would get to swinging it around and just beat the heck out of the other kittens. It got to where we had to take him away now and then so the other kittens got to eat. We left that cast on for about five weeks, and when we took it off, his leg was as good as new. The vet just shook his head and said he never would have believed it if he hadn't seen it with his own eyes. We had that old black cat for years. He followed us around just like the dogs did.

THE CAT CURE

WE HAD THIS young cat, probably one year old. Calico was his name. He definitely had something wrong with him. We went to the barnyard one morning, and there he was. His head was down between his front legs, and when he walked, all he could do was go backward. He was shaking, and his eyes were closed. We went and found Dad, and he looked at the cat and said, "You boys are going to have to put him down." We said, "OK." I know that this is hard for some folks to hear, but for all you folks that grew up on farms, you just knew about life and death at a young age. Just like us, you would try your best to save your animals, but sometimes, you just couldn't. So Doran and I got the cat. We wondered how we should do it. Doran got a good idea. He said, "No use wasting a twenty-two shell, so you hold him, and I will just use my bow." Well, it sounded all right to me, so I got a hold of the cat. Doran drew his bow back and shot the cat right behind the front legs. The arrow went through the cat and was hanging out both sides. I let go, and the cat took off. It ran between two apple boxes and broke the arrow off, and he was gone. Dad asked us later if we had taken care of the cat. We told him yes. Well, I felt kind of bad that we could not find the cat to bury him. Well, about four days later, here came Calico cat, walking straight as an arrow; no pun intended. The arrow was still hanging out both sides, but he was cured. The arrow finally rotted off or fell out, and the holes in his sides grew shut and haired over. We had old Calico for years after that, but he did run and hide if he saw Doran with his bow and arrow.

HIGH SCHOOL

S UMMER WAS OVER, and it was time for another chapter in
my life to begin. I had a unique set of circumstances. You see, the
street I lived on was the dividing line for two school districts. My side of
the street went to Trent Elementary; the other side of the road went to
Millwood Elementary. But when we went to high school, we all went to
West Valley High School. The church that I went to was in Millwood.
That is the church that sponsored our scout troop, so I knew kids from
both school districts. So when it came to the transition between grade
school and high school, it was easy for me because I knew so many of
the kids from both sides of the road. I was pretty sure that my days in
the principal's office were things of the past! After all, I was an adult now.
I had started high school. What could go wrong? So we got to our first
homeroom meeting, and I found out that we had to go to six different
rooms each day. That meant being on time six times a day and also having
six different teachers a day. I thought to myself, *I might have been a little
hasty in my thinking about the office and the adult part.* So hang on, and
you will see what happened. There were cars and girls, cars and girls, cars
and girls, and oh yeah, a little schoolwork too. I walked into school like
I owned the place, and it worked. I never got stuffed in a garbage can or
had my pants pulled down or any of that other crap that poor freshman
went through. OK, I did have a dead frog show up in my lunch once,
and all the senior boys laughed when they saw that. And somehow, my
gym trunks got the crotches cut out of them, and they were turned blue
from ink. And I did accidently get locked in my locker once until the
gym teacher missed me and let me out. All of these accidents happened in
the first week of school. I thought, *how can this many accidents happen to
such a savvy guy like me?* Well, of course, me being one of the best football
players to ever grace the grade school gridiron, I had to go out for high
school football. When I got to my first practice, I was surprised that
they wanted a football star like me to do push-ups and tackling drills. I
guess it was going to take the coaches a little time to find out how good I

really was. Now, this did take a lot more time than I had envisioned. This brings to mind a memory about the day I demonstrated to the coaches and my fellow teammates how tough I really was. At the time, I played right halfback, which meant I was a running back and pass receiver. I also played linebacker on defense. I know what you're thinking—how could a guy play both offense and defense? Well, in my day, you played both, or you probably didn't play at all. So we were at practice one day, and they called forty-one right, which meant that I went to the right sideline and went deep down field as a pass receiver. Now, this is where I showed everyone how tough I was. I was streaking down the right sideline, waiting for the pass. I had my arms out, ready to catch the football. I heard the coaches and players hollering, and I knew that this was going to be a great catch. Why else would they all be cheering so loudly? I was looking back over my shoulder, ready for the catch, when all of a sudden; I was hit by the biggest linebacker that ever played the game. OK, after I came to, I found out what really happened. I was streaking down the right sideline like I said. I was thinking so hard about catching the football that I kind of ran out of bounds and ran straight into a big old light pole, and it was lights out. Here is where the tough part comes in. After I came to, I was ready to jump right up and play football, but the coaches said, "No way. You're done for the day." As I left the field, I heard some nervous laughter. I think some of the guys were thinking that they were just not tough enough to play this game of football. But I thought that I would help them all I could to toughen up and be more like me. Hey, that's what a great tough football player like me does.

BIOLOGY

I TOOK BIOLOGY my first year. Why? I do not know. Let me say I liked my frogs alive, and there was a lot of homework to do, and as you know, that was just not my style. And to say that our biology teacher was a real sharp guy would not be quite accurate. Nice guy just had his brain around too much formaldehyde for too many years. I remember one time he had some goldfish that were supposed to be prime specimens that we were supposed to study and write about. One day, some of the guys and I were down at the Spokane River, just fishing and messing around. The river ran through the little town of Millwood. It's only about one mile from the school. The main road through Millwood crossed the river. We used to jump off the bridge there. The river had a dam about five miles downriver from Millwood, so the water was deep enough to jump from the bridge. As I was saying, we caught some perch about six inches long. I looked at them, and a great idea came upon me. I told the guys "Don't kill those fish. Put them in a bucket and keep them alive until Monday." Of course, the guys wanted to know what was up. I told them to just get the fish in before school started and meet me in the biology room. Monday morning, I met the guys, and they had the fish with them. They told me that they were caught by the vice principal coming through the doors, and he wanted to know why they were carrying a bucket of fish into school. Jim is another quick guy like me. He told the vice principal that they were bringing them to biology class because Mr. Cook wanted to teach us something and we volunteered to bring the fish. I think that might have been when our problems began. But Jim assured me that the vice principal bought his story. We went into the biology room. We filled the sink with water and carefully netted Mr. Cook's fish from the tank and put them in the sink. We then put the perch into the fish tank and took our seats just before the bell rang. Mr. Cook came in, and we all sat there with our best innocent looks on our faces. Well, the teacher started teaching, and he still had not noticed the fish yet, and we could not have that. So I raised my hand. Mr. Cook called on me, and I said, "Mr. Cook is something wrong with your fish? Look how much they grew overnight." He went over to the tank, and he said, "You boys are fooling me. There's no way those fish could grow that big overnight." Jim said, "Well, you must look at them. They are huge." So Mr.Cook did look closer, and he hollered, "These are not my fish. What happened to my fish?" Well, by this time, the classroom was going bananas, and so was Mr. Cook. He then happened to look over to the sink and saw his fish. He ran over to the sink, and for some reason, he pulled the plug, and his fish were swimming around to keep from going down the drain. Jim and I jumped up and put the plug back in and saved his fish. Now, did we get a pat on the back? Not exactly. We did eventually get a pat on the backside. Mr. Cook took Jim and me to the office, and he told the principal what he thought we had done. We sat there with a "we're innocent" look, and I thought we were going to get away with it. But then the vice principal walked in and proceeded to tell about catching Jim and the guys with a bucket full of fish that morning, saying they were going to the biology room. The principal said, "Stand up, boys. I am pretty sure you boys know the drill." We did. We bent over and grabbed our ankles.

MELVIN BROWN

SUMMER

WELL, I MADE it through my first year of high school. It was 1955, and I was working on farms around our place. I was fourteen years old and getting ready to have my first legal car. What? You want to know what a legal car is? Well, it has to meet safety standards, like the lights and brakes all working. But when you are not old enough to have a driver's license, then all that other stuff don't matter. We had an old 1938 Dodge pickup that we drove around the farm. I had been driving tractors from the time I was eight years old. So I had no trouble driving that old pickup just as soon as I could see over the hood, which was at about ten years old. I think the headlight on the driver's side worked, and the brakes worked on the fourth pump of the brake pedal. We drove it only in the daytime and planned our stops according to the speed and how many pumps of the brake pedal it would take to stop where you wanted to. We had a three-speed manual transmission, so when you pumped the brake pedal the first time, you pushed the clutch pedal in at the same time and shifted down one gear. This gave you more engine compression and helped slow you down. Awe, the whole process was as beautiful as any ballerina you would ever see. Now, I was not allowed to drive the truck on the main road, but I did know every dirt back road and trail in a forty-mile radius of our farm. Awe, those were the days. I could get where ever I needed to get and never have to get on the main road. Well, I almost never got on the main road. I remember one day when Pat and I were way up Big Creek when a rear axle broke on the old Dodge. You might say we were up a big creek without a paddle. We were both fourteen years old and sixty miles from home by the main roads but only thirty-five miles by the dirt roads we traveled on to get there. You ask how can that be. Well, let me explain it. We left the farm and went up Gozzer Road to Berma Road to Coeur d'Alene Mountain Road. Now, these roads are all gravel back roads. As long as it was not paved, it was fair game. When we got to the top of Coeur d'Alene Mountain, we went down the other side onto Kalarney Lake Road. Then we caught the Lemonade Peak

Road, and then went down the Beaver Slide Road to Fish Creek Road. We drove across Fish Creek and into the town of Calder, Idaho. Calder, Idaho, sits on the banks of the Saint Joe River. It has a general store and a post office all in the same building. That's it. Then from Calder, we took the Big Creek Road up to the end of the road, and that's how you do it when you're fourteen years old and can't drive on the main roads. We got out of the truck and wondered what we should do, and my buddy Pat said, "Well, its five miles down to old Rowdy's Ranch, so we might as well go fishing." We fished all the way down to old Rowdy's place. We had a whole string of fish. Now, we never could figure out if Rowdy's Ranch was a ranch or a junkyard. Either way, it was a great place. I think Rowdy had one of every pickup made in the last twenty years, but I think only two of them actually ran. We found old Rowdy out in the barn and told him what our problem was. Old Rowdy said, "Boys, we are in luck. I have got an old thirty-eight Dodge over in the trees there." I said, "Rowdy, I only have two bucks and a string of fish."

"Well, Melvin, that will be just about right. Let's get some tools and get to it." We got the axle out, threw it in old Rowdy's truck, and roared back up Big Creek. We got our truck fixed and headed for home, and I got there just before dark. I was glad of that because that headlight on the driver's side did not always work. Dad asked, "Where you been all day?" I said, "Oh, just over to Pat's place."

"Well, glad you're home because you have hogs to feed."

This was a logging road and how we got to Big Creek on the back side of Coeur d'Alene mountain. The lake in the lower right hand corner is named Killarney Lake.

MELVIN BROWN

TURNING GREEN

DAD DECIDED THAT we needed a new hog barn, so we set about building one. First, we poured cement for the reservoir under the building. You ask why any sane person would put a reservoir under a hog barn? Well, let me explain. You see, we built barns with slotted floors in them. Now, you ask what a slotted floor is. Well, a slotted floor sits atop the reservoir. The floors have four-inch-wide slats with a half-inch space between each slat. This allows all the messes from the hogs to go through the slots and down into the twenty-two-thousand-gallon reservoir, and then it is pumped out and spread onto the fields around our farm. So as I said, we had the barn all framed up and the metal siding on the walls, and I was ready to put the metal on the roof trusses. I got the first three sheets on, and we ran out of daylight. The next morning, Doran and I were ready to start putting the metal roof on when Dad said, "Listen to me. Don't try to put roofing on in this wind." Dad had to go to town. I thought about his last words. Then I thought, *I am the best metal-roof installer in northern Idaho or maybe the whole state of Idaho. And shoot, that wind is not blowing that hard.* I got Doran and said, "Let's start putting roofing on." Doran said, "Dad told us not to work in the wind." I said, "Yeah, but the wind is not blowing that hard. Trust me. We can do it." Doran said, "OK." Let me explain. These roofing sheets were eighteen feet long, and we had to take them up a ladder and then walk across the finished roof to lay down the next sheet. I got up on the roof and was walking along, holding the sheet of roofing, when all of a sudden, a huge gust of wind came along—one that I had not counted on. When the wind hit that sheet of roofing, it spun me around, and down I went. As I slid down that roof, I think you can guess what was flashing before my eyes again. As I went over the edge of the roof, I saw this big pile of old broken lumber and metal scraps that I was about to land on. I saw one small hole in this pile of stuff. I aimed my feet for that hole, and in I went. But when my feet hit the ground, I fell over, and my hands hit a piece of something and cut my finger pretty bad, then swish, that sheet of roofing sailed right over my head. So Mom took me to the doctor, and he stitched me up and gave me a new tetanus shot, and home we went. I went out to the shop, and I saw that I still had the farrowing crates that we were building for the new farrowing house to finish. Well, I thought to myself, *I should be able to weld these together even with this bad hand.* Those farrowing crates were made out of one-inch galvanized pipes, so as I started to weld, I noticed that there was a cold wind blowing through the doors. So I closed the shop doors and kept on welding. Now all of a sudden, I was not feeling well. I went in the house, and I looked in the mirror, and I was turning green. I was a sick puppy. I thought that between the cut finger and the tetanus shot and the fumes from the galvanized welding, these had almost done me in. When Dad came home and heard what had happened from Mom, Dad came into my room. He looked at me and said with great compassion in his voice, "Melvin, I told you not to put metal roofing on in the wind." You know, I think that Dad was starting to make more sense. I might just start listening to Dad one of these days.

THE NEEDLE

DORAN AND I were out in the farrowing barn, taking care of two new litters of baby pigs. Here's what we had to do with them: When the little pigs are born, we would give them an iron shot because these pigs were never out in the dirt, so you had to give them iron that they would have gotten naturally from the dirt. Then we would clip the sharp points of their teeth so they would not bite the sow while they were feeding. We would tie the umbilical cord and dip it in iodine. Now, each sow had seven to ten babies each and we had to do all of this to each one, so we were busy. In came our little brother Gordon and he was screwing around and giving us a hard time. I told him to knock it off. He just laughed and ran out of the barn. So we were back to work when Gordon came back in and started poking Doran and making a lot of noise, which started getting the sows nervous, and that's not good. I told him, "If you come in here again, I am going stick you in the butt with this needle full of Tyramicin." Now, these needles are not the same size needles that you get from your doctor. No, these are big hummers. Gordon just laughed and left again. I told Doran to give me an empty syringe, which he did, and I took the needle off. I told Doran that if Gordon came back in there, I was going to scare him with the syringe. He was going to think that the needle was on the syringe. Well, in he came and started messing around again, so I grabbed the syringe and jumped up. Gordon started running for the house with me right behind him. I hollered, "Get ready, boy. I told you what was going to happen." I reached out and touched him on the butt with the empty syringe. Gordon fell over in the yard and started screaming. Mom ran out and said, "What's wrong with him?" I said, "Dang if I know. He just fell down." Then Gordon screamed, "He shot me full of Tyramicin." Well, Doran was right behind, and I had the syringe behind my back. Doran reached out and took the syringe and slipped it in his pocket and walked away. I held out both hands, and I showed Mom that I did not have a needle on me. Mom looked at Gordon and told him to get up and quit acting like an idiot. She told Gordon,

"Your older brother can do some dumb things, but he would never shoot you full of Tyramicin." Well, later on, we talked to Gordon, and he told us that he felt the needle go into his butt, and he knew that I had given him a shot. So we came clean and told him what we had done, and we all laughed about it. Well, Doran and I laughed. Gordon not so much.

FOURTH OF JULY

I WANT TO talk to you about the Fourth of July and all the fun we had. Now, we did know that the Fourth was about our independence from England. This was back when they actually taught things like that. We had great parades. Now, you have never been to a parade until you have been to a small country town's Fourth of July parade. Every kid wanted to be in the parade along with their dogs and their bikes. They decorated their bikes with crepe paper and playing cards in their spokes to make a lot of noise. Then here came the fire truck with the firemen throwing candy to the crowd and using their sirens to make some noise. Then came the Shriners on their little motorized cars or bikes, doing various riding tricks. Awe, everyone loved the Shriners. Then the floats came along pulled by tractors and with the parade queen and her princess. Now, as I got older, I enjoyed this part more and more. Then along came the town ambulance—that is, if they had one, and they threw out more candy and squawked their sirens to make some noise. Then along came the horses. They were all sizes and colors and ridden by the farm kids and men and women, and everyone hooted and hollered and made a lot of noise. As you can tell, noise was a big part of the Fourth of July. Another phenomenal thing that would happen as the horses went by was they were always last because they always left a gift on the pavement, which us kids referred to as Tennessee road apples. Well, anyway, as I was saying, as the horses went by, the crowd would just fold in behind and form a new parade all the way through town. Then it was time for the picnic in the park. All the young mothers would show off their babies. And the proud grandparents would show off their new grandbabies. Meanwhile, us kids would be busy with—you guessed it—fireworks. So here are some of the great things we did with fireworks. We loved to find a red anthill and sneak up on it and plant firecrackers in the hill and then light them and blow up some red ants. But sometimes, the ants won the battle and got up your pants leg before you got your charge set. You ain't lived until you have your pants full of red ants—not good. Speaking of fireworks, now in my time, we had fireworks, not this crap they call fireworks today. We had lady-finger firecrackers, we had good two-inch firecrackers, and we had cherry bombs and good old M-80s. Also real Roman candles that actually shot gobs of fiery-colored stuff into the air. Oh yeah, we had sparklers, but that was for the girls to use. We boys took care of the heavy-ordnance stuff. We had whistling peats. They would spin around and around, throwing sparks all over the place and whistling and then *boom*. We had rockets with sticks on them. You just stuck them in the ground and lit the fuse. They went up to great heights and exploded and then rained hot stuff down on us. Neat. We also had small bottle rockets. You just put the stick into a pop bottle, and off they would go and *boom*. Sometimes, we just couldn't find what we were looking for at the fireworks stand, so we just made what we wanted. Here is one of the ones that we liked to make. We would hunt around the neighborhood and find two different-sized tin cans so that one fit inside the other. You then took the smaller can and punched a hole on the top that a two-inch fire cracker would just fit into. Then you took the bigger can and filled it half-full with water, then put the smaller can inside the bigger one and lit the fuse. The smaller can would take off like a rocket with a water trail behind it. You would only get about three turns before the smaller can would not fit into the bigger one. Then you had to find another can that fit. This was cool, but us guys wanted to go bigger, so I thought that if it could go that high with a two-inch firecracker, just think of what we could do with an M-80. Well, that sounded good to the guys, but coming from me, how could it not sound good to them? After all, I was the best heavy-ordnance guy in northern Idaho or maybe all of Idaho. So we got the cans and put a hole on the top that fit the M-80, filled the big can half-full with water, and lit the fuse. We stood there, watching, and *boom*, the whole thing blew up, and we were dodging tin shrapnel and hot water. I shook my head and said, "I guess that M-80 was too big, but dang, did you see that explosion? It was great." And the guys said, "Yeah, great."

DORAN'S PAINFUL TRICK

I REMEMBER ONE time, my brother Doran was lighting firecrackers in his hand and then throwing them in the air and watching them explode. Mom saw him doing that and told him to quit doing it, or he was going to blow his hand off. Doran explained to Mom that he knew what he was doing, and out the door he went. Five minutes later, he came running through the door, holding his hand and jumping up and down, crying. Here is what he told us happened. He lit the fuse, and it burned too fast, and as he threw it, it went off about six inches from his hand, thereby saving his fingers, but they were swollen for a few days. Mom said, "I told you that you were going to blow your hand off." Then Mom said, "Being that you didn't blow your hand off, go out and play." Well, Doran learned to use his other hand for a few days, and all was well.

THERE GOES THE TOES

I REMEMBER ANOTHER Fourth of July. I was fifteen at the time, and Ted and I were at the farm, and we had two sisters from down the road over for the day. Now, of course, we were both trying to impress these two sisters, and that's where the trouble began. Ted would do something like blow up a red anthill. Now, that got the girls' attentions, so I had to come up with a better one than that. Now, over the years, I have come to the conclusion that hormones and good sense are not compatible. So I told Ted, "Just put that two-inch firecracker on top of my boot just above my toes." Ted said, "You sure? That could be real hard on your foot." I said, "Naw, I'm tough." Oh, my girl just smiled, at least I thought she was my girl, but I think Ted thought the same thing. So Ted put the firecracker on top of my boot and lit the fuse. I just stood there with a big smile on my face as that fuse burned, and when that sucker went off, I thought that all my toes had been blown out the bottom of my boot. Ted and the girls were all looking at me. I just kept on smiling. They asked me, "Didn't that hurt?" I looked them right in the eye and said, "Nope." I walked off like I was going to the outhouse, and when I got behind the house, I fell down on the ground, rolled around, and 'bout wet my pants. It hurt that bad. Ted asked me later how it really felt. I told him, "I thought you blew my foot out through the bottom of my boot." He told me that I was good because the girls thought that I was the toughest, bravest man they had ever seen. That right there made it all worthwhile, but like I said, hormones and good sense don't mix well at all.

THE MAILBOX

CLIFF, PAT, AND I were driving my dad's car one day and just cruising around the lake when Cliff came up with a great idea. He said, "Let's put a firecracker in old Jack's mailbox." Now this was not the Fourth of July; it was late August. But we always made sure that we had enough fireworks leftover for special occasions like this one. Now old Jack lived in a shack on Arrow Point that runs out into Lake Coeur d'Alene. I think that the only times that Jack took a bath were whenever he accidently fell into the lake, which did not happen very often. Anyway, it seemed like a good idea at the time, so we pulled up and put a firecracker in old Jack's mailbox and lit the fuse. We took off down the road, and we were all looking back to see the firecracker go off. Guess what? The only thing that went off was us right off the road and down a ten-foot bank and into a tree with the left front fender hitting first. Now, this was not good. About this time, old John Gozzer came along on his Ford tractor. He said, "Looks like you boys ran off the road." Now, old John was a sharp one. He never missed a thing. So John hooked on to the car and got us pulled back up on the road. We pulled the fender away from the tire. We were only two miles from the ranch, so we drove home—a trip that I was not looking forward to. Just before we turned into the lane, I told Cliff and Pat, "You guys let me do the talking." Cliff said, "Well, you have a quarter of a mile to figure out what you are going to tell your dad." Leave it to Cliff to put the pressure on at a time like this, but I think that he knew I could handle it. Oh yeah, I forgot to mention that the radiator had a big old hole in it. We were steaming badly by the time we got home—not good. Well, Dad came out of the barn, took one look at his car, and said, "What happened?" Here's what I told him: "We were coming around the turn at Arrow Point, and here came this drunk driver on our side of the road, so what else could I do but run off the road." All Dad said was "Right." Then he said, "Your mother and I are going on a vacation in the morning, and I am going in this car, so I don't care how, but it had better be fixed by morning." Well, we went down to the wrecking yard and found an old green fender and a radiator. We got the old ones off and the new ones on just as Mom and Dad came out to leave on their trip. They had a gray car with a green front fender as they went down the lane. The three of us went to bed. I ran into Jack about a week later, and he said some young punks had put a firecracker in his mailbox and said he sure would like to know who they were. I said, "I will ask around, Jack, and if I find out who it was, I'll be sure to let you know." But you know I never did find out who put the firecracker in old Jack's mailbox. But you know, some mysteries are never solved. I remember the fireworks every Fourth of July that were set off over the lake. We would all go down to Arrow Point and watch them. Everyone would come down to watch them, and a great time was had by all.

TV

WELL, WE ALL heard about this thing called TV, but no one had seen one in our neighborhood. It was 1954, and things were about to change. Jake's dad went to a football game one night and bought a raffle ticket, and guess what? He won a sixteen-inch black-and-white Packard Bell TV. Now this was the first TV in the neighborhood for a year or more. So right away, Jake was a popular guy in the hood. We would all gather to watch this thing called television. It had rabbit ears, and you had to move them around now and then to get your picture just right. I am sure some of you old guys remember rabbit ears. But how many of you remember this. Jake's dad bought something that was supposed to give you color on the TV? What it actually was was a piece of cellophane divided into three sections—one red, one blue, and one green. You were to put it over your screen, and you would have color TV. But what really happened was you had three-colored people, houses, hills, etc. Jake and the rest of the gang loved to watch *Flash Gordon* every day at four o'clock. Well, guess what Jake's little sister loved? The *Howdy Doody Show*, and guess what? It came on at the same time as *Flash Gordon*. Now *Flash Gordon* was about spacemen and all the battles they fought in outer space. You might say that it was the forerunner for *Star Trek*. Now on the other hand, *Howdy Doody* was about a goofy clown that did not know his butt from his head. So as you can see, with one TV and two shows at the same time and all the boys against one little sister—not good. We boys would do everything we could to get little sister playing with her friends so she would forget about *Howdy Doody*. Well, we would just get into watching *Flash Gordon* when here came little sister saying, "I want to watch *Howdy Doody*." She would stamp her feet and cry until her mother would say, "OK, boys, let her watch *Howdy Doody*." I hated that clown. Can you blame me?

HIGH SCHOOL: SECOND YEAR

WELL, BACK TO school again, but I was looking forward to this year because I was old enough to get my driver's license. Now, that right there is a good reason to go back to school. So I went down to get my driver's license, and they handed me about a fourteen-page test to do. Now, this was way before computers and all that junk. You had to know all the hand signals. Yep, no electric turn signals and what all the road signs meant. Well, you guessed it: I flunked the first time around. For the life of me, being the great driver I am, I should not have had to take and pass a fourteen-page test. I went home in disgrace. I told Dad that I had flunked the written test. Dad looked at me, and this is what he said: "Son, maybe you should try reading the driver's manual like I tried to get you to do." I said, "But that's going take a long time to read all of it." And Dad said, "No longer than flunking that fourteen-page test every time you go in there. And if you flunk it three times, you then have to wait six months to take it again. It's your choice." I said, "Being that you put it that way, I guess I will read the driver's manual, but it just ain't right, me being the great driver that I am." Anyway, I finally passed the entire test and got that cherished piece of paper that said I could drive on the main roads. I guess Dad was right again. It was worth reading the driver's manual. But that night, the manual fell into the burning barrel and became a part of the purple haze.

THE DANCE

WELL, NOW THAT I had the driver's license and the fact that I had talked Dad into borrowing his car to go to the dance, life was good. As I said, I had talked Dad into using his car—not an easy task. He wanted to know where I was going and what time I was going to get home. I told him that I was going to the dance at the steel workers' union hall in Trentwood and that I would be home by midnight. Dad looked at me with that "I remember the drive-in movie thing" look in his eyes. I thought this could go either way, but then Mom stepped in and said to Dad, "How much trouble can he get into just going to the dance?" Dad looked at Mom and me and said; "Only time will tell." I got the car keys from Dad. He had a death grip on them, but I got them pried from his hand, and out the door I went before he could change his mind. I went over and picked Cliff up, and then we picked up Jim, and off we went, free and happy. We went out Trent road, but somehow, we missed the turn to the dance, which is hard to do because the union hall sits right on Trent road. So we thought what the heck? We might as well go on to Coeur d'Alene. It's only another twenty miles. We pulled into the Topper drive-in where all the cool people hung out. It did not take too long to find out that we were not quite cool enough to hang out at the Topper. Cliff got out of the car and started talking to a couple of girls. These two ugly-looking big guys came over and said to us, "If we were you punks, we would be leaving town *now*." We were out of town in five minutes, so we were heading back to the dance, and we missed the turn again. So Jim said, "Well, let's go to Spokane and tool the loop on Riverside." So we did. Well, we finally decided that we should go out to the dance so I could tell Dad that I was actually there, so back out to the valley we went. Just as we got to the dance hall's parking lot, the cops showed up and started searching cars for alcohol. Well, the Dugan boys had been doing some drinking, which, I might add, was not unusual for the Dugan boys. So they decided that they would leave before the cops could search their car, but they didn't want the cops to get their license plate number, so

Mike Dugan got on the back bumper to hide the plate and yelled for his brother Jimmy to go. Well, Jimmy went all right. He floor boarded the car. It jumped out onto Trent Road. But when he took off, he left Mike lying in the parking lot, so they arrested Mike and took off after Jimmy. It was not too hard to catch Jimmy because he went straight across Trent and into a ditch. After that was all over, we all went back into the dance. I found Jane just as they started playing "Love Me Tender." Now, that was some real belly-rubbing music, and Jane and I were good at it. Well, we danced, and when the dance was over, we thought that we should get something to eat. So we roared over to the local choke and puke on Pines Road. By this time, it was well after midnight, so I took Jane, Cliff and Jim home, and I went on home. The next morning when I got up, Dad was at the table, and he said to me, "Son, how far is up to the dance?" I told him three miles. And he said, "Then that would be a six-mile round-trip." I said, "Yep." Then Dad said, "I was just wondering how you put eighty miles on the car by only going six miles to the dance." I said, "Well, I had to pick Cliff and Jim up and then take them home." Dad said, "I didn't know that Cliff and Jim had moved out of state."

"OK, we might have gone a few places other than the dance. We had to eat." Dad said, "I know, son. I know it's hard to believe, but I was young once too." I said, "No, you were?" And we both laughed till we cried, then Dad said, "You better get your own car because you won't be using mine anymore." I said, "Funny you should say that because I have my eye on a one-owner jewel. He only wants fifty bucks for it." Dad just shook his head and went to work. It must have been something I said.

HIGH SCHOOL: JUNIOR YEAR

I T'S SCHOOL TIME again, and it's my third year of high school, so I think I will give you some of the highlights of this school year. One of those adventures comes to mind. One night, Cliff, Jim, and I were at the roller rink. We were in Cliff's car. We parked and went into the rink. Well, Cliff ran into Cheryl, and he had been trying to run into Cheryl for a long time. Well, it's time to go, but Cliff and Cheryl were nowhere to be found. We went outside, and yep, Cliff's car was gone. No problem. Jim and I just walked over to the railroad tracks. We did this quite often. We would wait for a slow-moving train to come by, and we would just hop on. We would ride up to the town of Dishman, and the train always slowed down there, and we would jump off and walk home. But for some reason, this train did not slow down, so we had to stay on it. Well, we ended up in Saint Regis, Montana, one hundred miles from where we wanted to be, in the middle of the night. We started hitchhiking. We got a ride down Lookout Pass into the town of Wallace, Idaho. We went into the local choke and puke and grabbed a burger. We ran into a guy who was going to Coeur d'Alene, and he gave us a ride. By that time, it was three in the morning. I got home just before four o'clock, so I was thinking, *How am I going to explain where I have been all night?* Then it hit me; it's four o'clock in the morning, and it's time to feed the hogs, so I just snuck out to the hog barn and started feeding the hogs. Well, Dad came into the barn and said to me, "First time you ever beat me to the barn to feed the hogs." I said, "Yeah, I didn't sleep too well last night. I got to thinking about you always getting up before me, and I just thought I should be more responsible for these poor pigs." Dad just looked at me and said, "I am glad that you are so dedicated to the hogs, but I don't think you need to dress up just like you are going to the roller rink," and that's all he had to say about that. Once again, thanks, Dad.

DORAN'S BIG BURN

I TOLD YOU that we cooked all our hog food. We had a barrel cut in half and mounted on legs so that we could have a fire under it to cook the pig food. We had to do this every day. Well, it was Doran and Gordon's turn to do the cooking. This took place in late July. It was eighty degrees outside. Doran was trying to get the fire started, but he was not having much luck. He went and got a gallon can of gas and started pouring it over the wood. Little brother Gordon told Doran, "I don't think that's a good idea." Doran said, "Trust me. I know what I am doing." Well, I don't know how many of you have seen the fumes that come from gas at eighty degrees, but there is a reason for No Smoking signs at gas stations. Back to Doran, he had all these gas fumes around him as he lit the match. *Boom.* I heard the explosion. I was in the barn. I started out the door just as Gordon came running up and said, "Doran blew up." I ran out just in time to see Doran lying on the ground. I could see that his back and arm were burned, but he was awake. I got him up and into the car and headed to the hospital thirty miles away. Doran was in no pain for the first twenty-five miles, but the last five miles was a different story. I got him to the ER, and they took him into the burn ward and started working on him right away, and I made the call to Mom and Dad as they were out in the truck on the road. I had to call to their next delivery point to find them. They rushed back to find Doran and me at the hospital. Doran was burned on his entire back and right arm. The doctor said it was a good thing that he did not have a shirt on, or it would have been so much worse. His face was not burned because he threw his right arm up in front of his face. At this time, the doctors said they had a new way to treat burns with no bandages, and they applied silver nitrate. He was in the hospital for two weeks, and when it was all over, Doran had no scarring anywhere. How's that for a miracle? I guess us Brown boys just lived right, or maybe we were the luckiest boys alive.

THE APPLE TREE

W E HAD AN apple orchard up on the hill above the farmhouse where every fall we picked bushels of apples and hauled them down to the house where Grandpa had his cider press. We would wash and then grind the apples up and then put them in the press and squeeze the juices out to make cider with. We grew wine sap apples that were tart, and then we mixed just the right amount of delicious apples in to give our cider a tart-but-sweet taste all at the same time. We then took all the leftover mash and dumped it in a strategic spot because the deer and bears loved to come down and eat the mash. Now, I ain't saying that this strategic spot had a clear field of fire, but we did eat a lot of deer meat and the occasional bear. We also had crab apple trees that Grandma made the best candy crab apples that you have ever tasted, not like the mushy canned ones you buy in the stores today. These were firm and sweet and *so* good.

Doran and I were up in the orchard one day, and we had this humongous apple tree. I don't know what kind it was, but it was big. I said, "I could climb clear to the top of that apple tree faster than anyone." Doran said, "I could climb just as fast as you." I said, "No way. You're too small, and I am the best tree climber in northern Idaho or maybe all of Idaho." So Doran said, "Watch this." Before I could stop him, he started up the tree, and dang, he was fast. Well, he got to the top of the tree, and he started to fool around, and I told him to knock it off before he fell. But he kept it up, hollering, "Boy howdy, did you see how fast I climbed this tree?" All of a sudden, the limb he was standing on broke and down through the tree he came. He bounced off this limb, that limb, and that other limb. He looked like the steel ball in a pinball machine. Finally, he hit the ground flat on his back with the wind knocked out of him. As he lay there, gasping for air, I could not help myself. I started laughing my head off. It was just too funny. Well, Doran started getting his breath back, and I saw this "I want to kick your butt" look in his eyes, and I thought I could make it to the barn before he got to his feet, so I left. By the time Doran hobbled down the hill and found me in the barn, he had decided not to kill me after I told him that he looked like the steel ball in a pinball machine. He could see how cool and funny that was. We laughed our heads off and we thought, *What a story to tell.*

Hauling apples to make cider

GETTING LUCKY

CLIFF CALLED ME one night and told me that he might have a chance to take Jenny out. I said, "Great. You have only been trying for three years to take her out. Why did she change her mind now?" Cliff said, "Well, I think that she finally found out what a great, caring, compassionate guy I am." I almost choked on that one. I asked Cliff, "OK, what's the real deal? Because it's not your charm because you have been turning the charm on for the last three years, and she doesn't even know you're alive and probably wishes you weren't." Cliff said, "Melvin that is cold. OK, I do have a slight problem—one that you can help me out with." Now, I knew right there that I should have said "Talk to you later" and hung up. But no, I kept listening. Here is what Cliff told me: "Jenny has her cousin staying with her, and she will go with me if I find a date for her cousin. And right away, I thought of you, old buddy, you being my best friend and all." I said, "Whoa, hold on, hoss. I ain't that good a friend to want to take a girl out sight unseen." Cliff said, "I have met her, and she is beautiful. I am telling you. She is smoking hot." I said, "OK." We were driving Cliff's Pontiac. We went over to Jenny's, and out came the girls, and I met Julie, and she was beautiful all right. Off we went to the motor inn drive-in theater. We got a spot right in the middle, halfway back from the screen. We got out of the car and headed for the snack bar. Of course, the walk to the snack bar was a long walk because you had to walk up and down every row of parked cars to see who's there. You absolutely had to make the walk, especially if you had a fine-looking girl hanging on your arm. Jim was there with Mandy, and Ted was there with Joan. Dick was there with his cheery '32 Ford Victoria. He had two girls with him. I tell you, that car worked wonders for him. Jenkins was there on his BSA motorcycle. He was just sitting there with the speaker hung on the handlebars. The Dugan boys were there in Jimmy's '49 Mercury. It is so low to the ground that you would have a hard time running over a frozen horse turd. Jackson and Jim were over, harassing two guys from Central Valley. That might get interesting before the night was over because the motor inn drive-in theater was on the West Valley side of the valley. Anyway, that's the way we looked at it. The fact that there was no drive-in theater on the central-valley side of the valley was too bad for them. Loran pulled in, and I said to Cliff, "When did Loran lower the back of his car?" Well, Loran pulled up and parked and motioned for us to come over to his car, so we all went over, and he told us to stand behind his car. We crowded around the back of Loran's car, and the trunk opened, and three boys and two girls came out of the trunk. And Loran's car was sitting level again. Roberta and Patty were walking around. No one knew what car they came in or, for that matter, what car they would leave in, but those two good old girls would find a ride. We made it to the snack bar and got the girls what they wanted to eat and drink, and we ran into Carl and Betty. They had been going steady since before they were born. Anyway, that's what we guys thought. Well, we got back to the car and watched the first movie, and then its intermission time, which meant walking to the snack bar again and then back to the car. We saw Yoder had showed up on his Triumph motorcycle, and he was parked next to Jenkins. But now, Roberta was on Jenkins's bike, and Patty was on Yoder's bike, and I thought, *Ain't love grand?* The second movie started, and it's time to start fogging up the windows, or anyway, that's what Cliff and I thought. Cliff and Jenny settled down in the front seat, and when I say *settled down*, I mean you could not see their heads above the seat anymore. So I thought Julie and I should settle down in the backseat, and we did. About halfway through the movie, the car started rocking, and I thought, *Dang, Cliff is getting lucky up in the front seat.* Well, the movie was over, and as we left the drive-in movie, Cliff turned on the radio, and this is what we heard. Spokane just had a 2.0 earthquake. Now, ain't that something? Here I was, thinking Cliff was getting lucky in the front seat, and Cliff told me later that he thought I was getting lucky in the backseat. But you know, the girls were beautiful, and we had a really fun time, so I guess you could say that we got lucky after all.

MELVIN BROWN

CARS

L IKE I SAID, I bought my first car for fifty bucks. It was a 1940 Ford sedan. It had a flat tire as soon as I got home. It burned a quart of oil every fifty miles, but oil was only twenty-five cents a quart. The speedometer did not work along with the oil and heat gauges. When you drove it down the road, it pulled hard to the right, but that was all right because the only brake that worked was on the left front. So when you pumped the brakes three times, the left front brake would grab and pull you to a nice straight stop. The camshaft was flat on number 3 cylinder and number 8 cylinder also. The radiator leaked a little, but you only had to add water every twenty miles or so. Not bad since water was free. The front window had a spider web crack on the passenger's side. One back window was gone, but that was OK because it was summertime and the living was easy. The front seat was gone, so I drove it home while sitting on an apple box. But I knew where there was an old Dodge seat, and with a little work, I could make it fit. But outside these few problems, she was cherry. I think Dad was impressed with my first car purchase because he just shook his head and walked away. I think he might have had tears in his eyes and did not want to try to talk, but I knew how proud he was that I had made such a great deal on my first car. Well, I drove that car about a month and thought that it was time to trade up, but no one on the upside wanted to trade for my '40 Ford, so I found a kid who really wanted a '40 Ford sedan.

He had a 1936 Ford coupe he wanted to trade. So I told him that well, I could do that, but I would be going downhill from my '40 Ford to his '36 Ford, so I would have to have fifty bucks and his car. Man, the kid jumped at that deal. He was moving up four car years. What a deal. Man, I was driving the '36 around. I found out that it had cable brakes, and the cables were stretched out. It did not work to pump the brakes. You just stomped the brake pedal to the floor and started shifting down and, in an emergency, left the brake pedal on the floor and left the clutch pedal out and turned off the key. Worked every time. Now, the '36 Ford had a canvas square in the metal top, and when the fall rain started, it rained as hard inside as it did on the outside. So I thought to myself, *it's time to do some car buying again.* Now, I was working in an aluminum foundry after school and in the summertime, so I had money. After all, I was making two dollars and fifty cents an hour, so I was looking to upgrade my mode of transportation.

So I started looking around the vast car market, and I finally found just what I was looking for. It was a nice 1951 Chevy. The tires actually had some tread on them—well, three of them did. The left front tire's tread was scrubbed off and had a slight misalignment problem, but it could be easily fixed with some wrench work and a big hammer. I thought, *I can fix that.* And the guy selling the car said to me, "Yeah, I could have fixed it myself. I have just been too busy. That's why I am giving you such a great deal on this car." Well, right there I knew I had me another great deal. I just don't know how I get the great cars like I do. This car had a few problems, like the heater worked all the time—winter or summer, it ran on high heat. The locking handle on the passenger-side wing window was gone. What's that? You wonder what a wing window is. Well, in the old days, the cars had a little triangular window in front of the roll-down door window. They called them the wing windows. You could open them, and they would suck wind in from the outside to cool you down and to help defrost the windshield. But if the locking handle was broken, like mine was, the wing could do whatever it wanted. But those things were all fixable, so I made the deal. You might say I stole that car for two hundred bucks. Whoa, Dad would be proud of his son's business abilities. This brings me to another one of those Keystone Kops moments in my life, so as I tell you this story, you just imagine an old Keystone Kops movie.

LOWERING MY CAR

S O I HAD been thinking about raking my car; this means lowering the front end so low that you had to be careful driving over frozen horse crap, or you would hit your bumper. So anyway, I was talking to Jenkins about it, and he said, "Hey, bring it over to my place Saturday, and we will lower that puppy, and we will put that split manifold and duel pipes on at the same time." I said, "OK, what time do you want me there?" Jenkins said, "Oh, about one o'clock." I started over to Jenkins's place at one, but I ran into Jim. We talked for a while. And then I ran into Sue and Jane, and we talked for a while, and just like that, it's four o'clock. When I got to Jenkins's place, he said, "Glad you could make it." So Jenkins's driveway was gravel and not exactly level, and we only had one hydraulic jack, so we jacked the passenger side up and pulled the tire off. Jenkins said, "I will take the A-frames off and take the torch to the coil spring. Why don't you climb under and start putting the new pipes on?" So I was under the car, working on putting the new exhaust pipes on, when I felt the car starting to slide off the jack. I hollered, "The car's falling," but it's too late. The car slid off the jack and fell on me. It came down across my abdomen. It hurt bad, but as Mel Browns, luck would have it, I was just thin enough that I was not totally mashed. Now, the other frame member was right above my head, but that was the side that still had the tire on the front end, so it kept the frame about two inches above my head. Here's where the Keystone Kops come into my life again. I was pinned under the car and was being quite vocal about wanting out from under it—*now.* Jenkins's mom and dad and sister heard all the noise out in the driveway and came running out. About this time the trouble light got kicked out, so now it was pitch-black. Nobody could see anything. Jenkins got the jack back under some place on the car and jacked the car back up, but just as he started to try to pull me out, I felt the car moving, and I hollered, "It's going to fall again." Jenkins's dad went to the front of the car and started to push, but this just happened to be the wrong way to be pushing. Jenkins's mom and sister ran to the back of the car and started pushing in the right direction. They pushed with all their might. But guess what? Jenkins's dad was much stronger than the two women, so yep, you guessed it; he pushed the car off the jack and back on me. Now, I was getting tired of holding this car up, and it wasn't hurting any less every time it fell on me. Somehow, they got the light working again, and Jenkins got the jack just right and jacked the car up, and his dad grabbed my legs and pulled me out from under the car. They called an ambulance, and off I went to the hospital again. Well, I was a grease ball from one end to the other. Now, my mother came in and saw that the white sheets they had me lying on had turned black. She said that she was glad that I was alive, but she said that she sure wished I had had clean shorts on. Well, a few days later, we got the car back together, and it was way cool.

My most favorite car that I have owned was a 1937 Ford coupe. It was the first eighty-five-horsepower flathead that Ford built. They only built six hundred of them in '37. I drove that car for two years, then like an idiot, I sold it for seventy-five bucks. What can I say? I had my eye on a cherry '53 Studebaker.

THE PAINT JOB

I REMEMBER ONE time, old John had the ugliest '41 Ford coupe that any of us had ever seen. Both front fenders were a different color—the right front fender was blue and the left one was green. The trunk lid was white, and the rest of the car was yellow—ugly. We kept telling John that he had to get that car painted, or we were going to paint it for him. John said he would do something about it, but he never got around to it. So we thought we would teach old John a lesson. Now, I guess today it would be called bullying, but back then, it was just having fun. Now, you have to know that John was a farm boy, and he liked a good joke as well as the next guy. So anyway, one morning, we brought a gallon of red barn paint and a broom, and we painted John's Ford—windows and all. Well, John came out for lunch. He looked at his car. He went over and scratched the paint off the windows and turned around and said, "I like it." You know, John drove that car the rest of the school year. For the rest of the school year, we wondered who the joke was really on. I don't think it was on John.

THE WRECK

I THOUGHT THAT I should build this high-strung go-kart, so I did. I welded up the frame and built the steering, and it turned a little bit quick, but I figured I could handle it all right. I found a big old McCulloch chain saw motor and got it mounted and all tuned up, and I was ready to go. My buddy Pat was over to see how it would run. I went screaming down the lane and out onto the road. I headed out toward the general store. I turned around at Gozzer Road and started back, so I thought that I should try some handling test. I got out in the middle of the road, and I started weaving between the broken white lines. Well, the first couple of passes went OK, so I picked the speed up and zipped through the next break, and the steering kind of grabbed a bit. But I was already into the next break when it really grabbed, and it almost threw me out butt first onto the pavement. So I grabbed hold of the steering wheel to keep from being thrown out, but in doing that, I jerked the wheels to the left, and off the road I went. I went up a steep bank and then rolled upside down and landed in the middle of the road with the go-kart on top of me. Now, crash helmets were not in vogue at that time, if you could even find one. So wouldn't you know it, I got two big cuts in the back of my head. I got out from under the kart and pushed it off the road and started running back to the ranch. I got to the lane, and I couldn't go any farther. Pat was there with my car, so he put me in the car and took off to Coeur d'Alene, twenty miles away. We got into town, and I sort of passed out by this time, and Pat did not know where the hospital was. I use the term *hospital* loosely as there was just this tiny brick building and one doctor. Well, anyway, this cop came driving by, and Pat did the only thing he could think of: he gave the cop the international finger sign. Well, that worked. The cop turned around and pulled us over, saw the shape I was in, and said, "Follow me." We got to the hospital, and the doctor sewed me up and turned me loose. Two days later, I was sicker than an old cur dog. I went to our family doctor in Spokane. He looked me over and said I had a bad infection because they had stitched me up hair and all. I got better and started thinking about the go-kart, and I thought I could get that steering fixed right. But when I went out to the shop to look the kart over, the wheels and the motor were gone. *Now,* I wondered, *who would do that to a perfectly good go-kart?*

SCHOOL LUNCH AND THE TRACTOR

THIS WAS WAY back before you had to eat a good lunch. I remember the school gave us a piece of white bread with lots of butter and a piece of whole wheat bread on top so that we got all our daily requirements all in one sandwich. They also served the worst scalloped potatoes in the world. And of course, there was mac and cheese. Anyway, I think it was real cheese. But they always gave us a container of whole milk to round out our healthy lunch. So knowing all this, there was only one thing we could do. And that was to leave the school grounds and drive a mile down the road to Joe's Pizza. The lunch bell would ring, and we were out the door and into our cars and off to Joe's Pizza. Aw, Joe's was a first-class place. It had about five tables and twenty square feet of floor space to walk around in. There was no ventilation to take the cigarette smoke and pizza smell out of the building. And then there was the jukebox and fifty teenagers all at once, talking, laughing, and singing along. Joe could have made his pizza out of anything. It would not have mattered because it was the place to be at lunchtime. So as I said, we would load up our cars and let them duel pipes roar as we made our way out past the principal's office and down the road to Joe's Pizza. One day, a memo came down to all the students. This is what it said: there will be no cars leaving the school grounds at lunchtime—signed by the principal himself. So the next morning after the memo came down, my buddy Dick came driving into the school's parking lot in his dad's 9N Ford tractor. So us guys all gathered around Dick and asked what's up. Dick said, "Well, boys, the memo don't say nothing about tractors." I always thought Dick was a little slow, but this was a brilliant observation on Dick's part. Well, at lunchtime, we piled fifteen guys onto Dick's tractor, and out we went, right past the principal's office and down to Joe's pizza. Well, that afternoon, another memo came down, and this is what it said: there will be no tractors leaving the school grounds at lunchtime or any other form of transportation that you can think of—signed by the principal himself. You know I always thought that our principal had no sense of humor, but he was beginning to prove me wrong. A few weeks later, I found out for sure. Here is how that went.

THE PRINCIPAL OF THE THING

I T WAS FRIDAY afternoon. Cliff, Jim, and I had decided that we needed to start the weekend early, so we left right after fourth period. We thought we would walk over to the bowling alley and see what was going on over there. Just as we walked up to the corner of Argonne and Sprague, the light turned red, and guess what? The principal drove up and stopped right in front of us. Now, this was an embarrassing situation to say the least. My buddy Cliff was never accused of being shy, so he walked over to the principal's car; his windows were down. Cliff leaned down and said, "We won't tell on you if you don't tell on us." Cliff stepped back. The light turned green, and the principal drove off, and we went on to the bowling alley. Monday morning, we went to school and waited for the worst. We never heard a word about our encounter. Just like that, I knew that our principal had a great sense of humor and was an all-around good guy. Does that mean that I got away with anything I wanted to with him? Not on your life. I think that it was just that one time we all went away laughing, and that's the stuff you just don't forget.

THE FIGHT

I WAS IN the hall, talking to the boys, when Jerry came up to me and said, "I hear you've been messing around with Robin."
"I'll tell you what, Jerry, if Robin was the last girl on earth, I would not be messing around with her." The guys started laughing, and I don't think that helped the situation at all. So I thought I would help Jerry out, and I said, "Jerry, you are a friend of mine, and if Robin is your girlfriend, then you have all the trouble and misery you need." This did not seem to make Jerry feel any better. By this time, the guys were just laughing and waiting to see what was going to happen. It did not take long to find out. Jerry said, "I will see you after school, out behind the gas station. We are going to settle this once and for all." Now, my back was up against the wall, so I said, "Jerry, Jerry, I don't want to have to whip your butt, but you are not leaving me any choice, so I guess I will be there after school." Four o'clock and we were all out behind the gas station. Jerry and I squared off, and I said, "Jerry, we don't have to do this." But Jerry charged at me, so I hit him, and dang, that hurt. I find out later that I broke a bone in my hand. Well, Jerry swung at me, and I was able to duck out of the way. He hit a car and broke a bone in his hand. And just like that, the fight was over, and we went home. Mom dragged me over to our doctor's office. She talked to Doc without me in the room. Then they brought me in, and the doctor got a hold of my hand and started setting it, and he said, "Do you really like fighting?" So I told him, "Right at the moment, not so much." Every time I would start to pass out, the nurse would put smelling salts under my nose just so I could stay awake to enjoy all of this. I decided right then and there that I was a lover, not a fighter. Through all of this, Jerry's parents and mine did not file lawsuits or blame each other's kid. They just said to us, "Did you two idiots learn anything?" Monday morning, I went to typing class with my cast on. The teacher looked at me and said, "Why do boys fight?" I said, "That is a very good question to which I have no answer." In the meantime, Robin, who started this

whole thing, dropped Jerry and took up with Danny, whom Jerry and I always thought was a real dork. We thought, *better him than either one of us*. We both decided that it was going to take a lot longer to understand girls than we originally thought.

THE KAYAK EPISODE

MY BROTHERS AND I were the best kayak builders in northern Idaho or maybe the whole state of Idaho. None of this fancy plastic things that you see nowadays; no, ours were wood frames with canvas covers painted to waterproof them. They weighed half what the new plastic ones weighed. Well, Doran and I had just finished our newest kayak. It was twelve feet long, and we could not wait to try it out. But we did not want to just put it on the lake. No, we wanted to try it for the first time on the mighty North Fork of the Coeur d'Alene River. We planned to take Highway 90 over Fourth of July Canyon to the Kingston exit and then up the river to Prichard and put it in there and float down to the Snake Pit Restaurant for our take-out spot. We got the kayak tied to the roof of Doran's old Ford Galaxy. We were a little short on rope, but with my great rope-tying ability, I knew it would hold. We got to the top of Fourth of July. The reason they call it that is because it took so much dynamite to build the road. Well, over the pass we went and down the other side. Well, Doran was picking up speed. He got that old Ford doing about seventy. All of a sudden, we heard this strange noise. I asked Doran, "Hey, what do you suppose that noise is?" Doran said, "Danged if I know." About that time, we heard the boat leave the top of the Ford. I looked out the back window, and the boat was in the air. I was amazed at how aerodynamic that boat was. It floated left, then it floated right, then left and right, but it was losing altitude rapidly. The main problem was the car that was behind us was swerving and trying to figure out which way our kayak was going to go. Well, just as the kayak hit the road right in front of the car, the guy swerved but not quickly enough and he ran over the end of our boat. We all got stopped, and I figured that we were about to get a real chewing out from this guy. Doran jumped out of the car and went up to the guy, and this is what he said: "Man, you ran over my boat." The guy said, "Dang, I'm sorry. I tried everything I could to miss it." Doran said, "Well, don't let it happen again." He said, "I sure won't." He jumped in his car, and he was gone. We threw the kayak off to the side of the road and beat feet for home before that guy changed his mind. But you know, I was real proud of my brother Doran. He jumped right in there and used everything I had taught him over the years. He took command and applied the right amount of BS at the right time to get us out of a tight spot.

THE SAINT MARIES RIVER RUN

MY BROTHER GORDON and I had a new kayak that we had just built and thought that we should go run the Saint Maries River in early June. That might have been our first mistake because we had a heavy snowfall that winter, and the rivers were still running hard. But we could not wait any longer to get on the water in our new two-man kayak. We got the kayak in the pickup, and off we went to Saint Maries and out Highway 3 toward Clarkia, Idaho. We came to the river just north of the town of Santa, Idaho; this was where we put the kayak in for our thirteen-mile run. We started down the river, and about a mile downriver, we hit something sharp and ripped a hole in the bottom of our kayak. We made it to shore and wondered what to do. There were railroad tracks along the river, so we walked back to the truck and drove up to Ted's house. But of course, Ted was not home because he was supposed to pick us up on the other end. So we borrowed Ted's twelve-foot aluminum rowboat. We drove back to the river and put the boat in and floated down to where the kayak was. We tied it on to the back of the rowboat with the good part floating in the water, and off we went. Well, we were doing OK when we came around Dead Man's Corner, and we found out why they called it that. You have heard of class four rapids, which are the worst rapids. Well, these must have been class twelve rapids. The water grabbed hold of that kayak and dragged it under our rowboat and turned us backward—not good. I yelled at Gordon to cut it loose, and he did, and I started rowing and finally got us straightened out, and we made it through the Dead Man's Corner alive. Well, that was bad, so we figured it couldn't get any worse—wrong. We came around the bend and into "you ain't going to make it alive" rapids. We fought those rapids for the better part of a mile. The boat was half-full of water, so we found a sandbar where we could pull the boat out and tip it over to drain it. Now, by this time, little brother had all the river running he wanted for the day. So me being the big brother, I took it upon myself to explain to my little brother that we were out in the middle of nowhere. We were soaking wet, and nightfall was not too far away. I told him I ain't ever had hypothermia, but I could see it coming if we did not keep going. Well, we got back on the water and went along for two miles with no problems. I knew that we were about to get to the pickup point. All of a sudden, we came to Killer Rock Rapids. It is a long chute that drops down fast and then swings around a blind corner. Just around the bend stands Killer Rock right in the middle of the river. Now Gordon is in the front of the boat, looking out for rocks, but he didn't have any trouble seeing Killer Rock because we hit it dead-on. Well, this was where my little brother walked on the water. That's right; that is the only way I can explain what happened next. When we hit the rock, Gordon went out over the bow and into the river. He had a hold of the boat with one hand, but the next thing I knew, he was back in the boat. The only way he could do that is to have walked on the water. I ain't lying. Well, after all this, it was dark, but the river was good, and we were floating down, wondering where Ted was going to pick us up. All of a sudden, we saw a ranch house, and Ted's pickup was in the driveway, so we pulled over and went up and knocked on the door. The lady of the house let us in, and there sat Ted eating elk steak. He said, "You boys look plumb tuckered out. You must have had a real good run on the river." I told him, "Yeah, it was a piece of cake. I thought the river would be up this time of year. Shoot, it weren't nothing." But you know, over the years, I have tried to get little brother to run the Saint Maries River again. He just starts shaking and saying that he ain't ever running that river again, especially with me.

SLATE CREEK AND COUSIN DAVE

WELL, COUSIN DAVE was over from the coast and on the farm for the summer, so we decided to take a couple of days and run up to Slate Creek to do some fishing. So brothers Doran and Gordon, Cousin Dave, and I got the pickup truck loaded, and off we went. We drove to Saint Maries, Idaho, and then up the Saint Joe River. We crossed the Saint Joe River at the Slate Creek ranger station. Now the ranger station sits on a small flat piece of ground. You cross that small flat piece of ground, and that is where the Slate Creek Road starts. At the bottom of this road is a sign that says "This road is not recommended for public use (use at your own risk)." Now, that right there is the kind of sign we boys love to see because it cuts way down on traffic. Because the Slate Creek Road is straight up and made out of loose slate shale and it is one lane, so no traffic is good. This is just the type of road that leads to some outstanding trout fishing. So off we went up the mountain, and halfway up, we met another truck coming down, so we stopped and talked to the guys. They had been there for a week and had caught fish until they were tired of catching them. We were the first people they had seen all week, so once we got by them, we had the whole creek to ourselves. Well, we started backing up and got as far up the bank as we could. The other truck started to go by us, and its hind wheel started to go over the edge. Now, this is not good as the edge is about five hundred feet above the creek. So I was able to inch ahead some, and then we got a come-along hooked to their front bumper and went up the bank and hooked it to a big old spruce tree. We put tension on the front end of their truck. Then I got my Handy Man jack out, and I jacked up the back end of his truck, and then we all pushed it off the jack. This moved the truck more toward the center of the road. We did this about four or five times, and their truck was back in the road. We all said good-bye, and off we went. We wound down the other side of the mountain and got back down to the creek. We got our tents all set up and a fire going and cooked some dinner. Next morning, we ate and went fishing. Cousin

Dave started fishing in this deep hole, and the rest of us were going to churn and burn on down the creek. Dave said, "Go ahead. I'm going to fish this hole for a while." This was where Cousin Dave had a spiritual experience. How you ask? Well, we were about a quarter of a mile from where Dave was fishing, and this took us the better part of an hour to get there. I was fishing, and all of a sudden, I turned, and there was Dave standing right behind me, and he wasn't looking too good. So I asked him what's going on, and all he could say was "*B-b-bear.*" So we got him calmed down, and he told us that he was fishing, and he got a funny feeling, and he looked up on the bank right above him, and there was a big old black bear sitting there, looking at him. Now, this is where Dave's spiritual experience happened because I figured he had to have walked on the water to get down the creek that fast. Dave said that I might be right because he couldn't remember how he got there. As I said, it took us about an hour to get down the river, and as near as we could figure, it only took Dave about fourteen seconds to cover the same distance. Cousin Dave told us that it was the biggest black bear in northern Idaho or maybe the whole state of Idaho. Forty-five years later, that bear ain't getting any smaller, according to Cousin Dave.

SIMMONS CREEK AND BAD CAR BRAKES

WE WERE CAMPED up on Simmons Creek, which runs down from the Montana border and into the Saint Joe River. I was driving my old '49 Studebaker pickup with a beautiful plywood camper on it. Well, OK, it was just a plywood box with no windows, but you could sleep in it and sort of stay dry when it rained. Well, when we drove into the spot where we stayed on Simmons Creek, there was a pile of brush in the way, so I just drove over it. No sense getting out and moving it. After all, I was driving a truck. We parked and got camp set up and went fishing. We caught some nice trout for supper and sat around the campfire, telling tales. Doran told us about the time he almost burned our barn down when he built a fort in the attic of the barn. He used gunnysacks to wall in his fort. Trouble was he hooked them up to the smokestack from the woodstove that was in the room below his fort. Well, needless to say, the first time I started the stove in the fall, all those sacks caught on fire, but we had running water at the barn, and we were able to put it out, thus saving the barn and Doran's butt because Dad did not find out about it. I proceeded to tell them about one time up on Big Creek. I was walking along the trail when I saw a big old yellow jacket nest. It's hanging about four feet high, right in the middle of the trail. There was no way around it. The creek has a deep hole on one side and a sheer rock wall on the other side. So I decided that I would just get down on my hands and knees and slowly crawl under the nest. Now, with all I know about yellow jackets, I knew that they wouldn't see me, so off I went. I got right under the nest, and you guessed it—*whap*, right in the back of the head. So right then and there, I knew that the time for crawling was over. I jumped up and headed for the creek. In I went, and it was deep and cold, so as I drifted downstream, I found myself on the wrong side of the nest again. So I being the smart guy that I was, I decided to fish downstream to the truck. Not to be outdone, Doran told about the time we were packing with the horses into the Mallard Larkin wilderness area in Idaho. Doran was leading our horse Cricket, and I was leading another horse. We had pack saddles on both horses. We had just crossed over Sawtooth Creek and started up the trail to Skyland Lake. We were up high on the side of the mountain when Cricket decided that she would get plum stupid for some unknown reason. She started bucking, and here was Doran trying to hold her so that she didn't go off the trail. Well, he kept her from going off the trail all right. But in so doing, she got off center, and she fell and pinned Doran up against a big old stump. Doran hollered, "She got me," so now I figured he had a broken leg or ribs, and we were four miles from the truck—not good. Cricket was on her side, thrashing around. She had one foot through one of the pack boxes, and she couldn't get up. I cut the pack saddle loose and got her leg undone. Cricket got up and started eating grass like nothing happened. Doran sat up by the stump, and I started checking him out. His legs worked. His ribs were a little sore but not broken as near as we could tell. So we decided that we may as well go on the two miles to the lake. But before we could do that, we had to make repairs to the pack saddle and get it back onto Cricket, which, I might add, she was not too fond of at this time. We started picking stuff up. It was strung all over the mountainside, but we got it all packed up, and off we went. Then Doran said to the guys around the campfire, "Boy howdy, we had us a grand old time, didn't we, bro?" I said, "Yes we did, little brother, yes we did." Then Dave had to tell about that rat hunt we had at the dump where he plastered that big-assed rat on brother Gordon's chest. The guys howled about that one. Then I had to tell them about the time Ted and I were down on the Selway River where Moose Creek comes in. We made camp and got ready for supper. I got a fire going, and Ted got into his pack and brought out this small jar of freeze-dried coffee. Now, this was way back when freeze-dried coffee had just come on the market. Well, he got his old coffee pot out and got the water boiling. He dumped that jar into the pot and let it boil. So we got supper ready and sat down to eat. Well, Ted poured himself a cup of coffee. He took a big sip, and his feet started stomping on the ground. I thought he might have been having a stroke or something. His eyes finally got uncrossed, and he got a breath, and he said, "What was that that I just drank?" I said, "That was that freeze-dried coffee that you wanted to try out. I take it you did not like it much?" Ted said, "I have never in my life tasted anything that bad." Well, we got to looking and reading the label on that jar, and in fine print, it said that the jar makes forty-five cups of coffee. We were camped there for about five days, and Ted watered that coffee down every day, but he never got it thin

MELVIN BROWN

enough to drink. Well, after that story, the guys around the fire could not take any more, so we called it a night and all went to bed. Next morning, we broke camp and planned to fish the Saint Joe River down toward Saint Maries, which is about sixty miles down the road from Simmons Creek. So I started down the slope from camp to the road. I put the brakes on, and I didn't have any brakes, so I turned the truck hard and ran into the bank to stop. Well, we got out and started checking things out. Do you remember that brush pile I told you about that I drove over? Well, that brush pile jumped up and tore the right front brake line off. Now, we were one hundred miles from home with no brakes. The guys wanted to know what we were going to do. I told them we were going to drive home and fish the Joe on the way down just like we planned. Little brother Gordon did not like the sound of this. Ain't it funny that every time he and I get right in the middle of a great adventure, he wants to bail on me? So I asked him, "Don't you know that I am the best driver in northern Idaho or maybe the whole state of Idaho?" He gave me this look that said that he was not aware of that fact. We started down the road. Now, there were no stop signs or much traffic, so there was no problem. If we saw a pool that we wanted to fish, we would just shift down and then turn the key off and coast to a stop before going off the road and into the river. Now, Cousin Dave was a little nervous, so he was sitting on top of the camper, keeping watch and hollering down, "Don't hit anything." All of a sudden, Dave hollered, "Stop. Look at that pool. Let's fish." I hollered, "How am I going to stop?" Dave said, "Hit the bank." So I did, and as we hit the bank and stopped, Dave flew off the camper, down over the hood, and was down at the river, fishing before the rest of us got out of the truck. That boy had his priorities straight. He took a chance on dying just to catch the first fish of the day. Now, folks ain't that what life is all about? Fish first; worry about the other stuff later. We got into Saint Maries with their one stop sign. We shifted down, turned the key off and coasted to a stop. Then we started the truck up again and turned right and headed for Harrison, Idaho, which has no stop sign. So we just crawled through town and went on home. All of us guys thought that it was one of our better trips, and it gave us all a great story to tell for years to come.

THE YEAR 1959 AND FREEDOM

IT WAS 1959—MY last year of my formal education. All I had to do was make it through this school year, and I would be free of this learning stuff—at least that's the way I saw it at the time. I thought maybe I should take Spanish just in case I happened to end up in Mexico sometime. Well, I started Spanish class, and it just didn't look right to me. I mean, who wants to talk like that? When I mentioned this to the teacher, she got upset with me and started sputtering something in Spanish, which of course, I could not understand. Well, anyway, after two weeks in her class, I had all I could take, and the teacher was on my case one day. Here is what I told her: "You know, I don't mind you chewing me out, but if you can't do it in English, then we don't have anything to talk about." That probably was not the best thing to say to her as she came unglued, and I took my usual trip down the hall to—you guessed it—the principal's office. The principal said, "I guess you don't like Spanish, so I am placing you in another study hall. Why? I don't know because you don't have anything to study, but I will say that you do it well."

Mel 1959 Graduation

Jamie, Mel and Ted
1959 Graduation

THE SCHEDULE

HERE IS MY school schedule for my last year. I had woodshop for first period, where I got straight A's. Then second period, metal shop, also straight A's. Third period was study hall. I needed that to wind down from the first two classes, and besides, I had to get ready for lunch. Back from lunch, fourth period was sign shop—yep, straight A's. Fifth period, study hall again. I had to get ready for sixth period, which was history and government class. I could hardly keep up with the bookwork. Now, at the end of the year, we had to take a test in government class. We were to start at the top of the government and name all the parts of the state government. Well, I got the governor down, and then my mind went blank. Just like that, the time for the test was up—not good. Of course, the teacher told me to stay after class. He said, "Melvin, couldn't you at least have put the lieutenant governor down on your list?" I told him, "You know, I knew that I forgot something." Now the bad news is if I flunked this test, I would be a half credit short of graduating. So I asked him, "Are you going to make me come back for one semester?" Here is what he said to me: "Heck no. I have had you for four years. I am going to give you D+, and you will be out of here." I thanked him and told him that he was my favorite teacher, which I really meant, but I ain't sure he believed me. But what the heck, I was free, and there was the whole world out there just waiting for me

SAT

I REMEMBER WHEN the people came to school to give the SAT test for college. They were testing ten kids at a time. As the day wore on, I still had not taken the test, which, I might add, had no appeal to me. Let me be a little more specific about that. You see, I had been working on our own farm from the age of eight. I know that sounds terrible to all the young granola crunchers reading this today, but I thought it was great. I went on to work for the farmers all around our farm. I mowed lawns and irrigated corn during two different summers. In high school, I worked in aluminum foundries after school. I worked in gas stations. Yeah, this was way back when we pumped your gas for you and checked your tires, oil, and water too. We did all of that for thirty-five cents a gallon for your gas. I am seventy-two years old, and I have never been on unemployment or welfare. I worked for other people and for myself my whole life. I told you all of this to finish the story about the SAT test. You see, my homeroom teacher knew me pretty well, and so when the guy came in to get me for the test, the teacher said, "Mr. Brown does not wish to take the SAT test." The test guy said, "Well, he can't get into college without the test." The teacher said to the guy, "I don't think that will be a problem for Mr. Brown." I looked at the teacher, and we both started laughing, and I thanked him for saving my butt. Now, I know that they will tell you that you can't survive without a college education, but I did. I have lived and worked in some really great places: Idaho, Washington State, Alaska for thirty years, Hawaii, and Oregon, and I never saw where a college education would have done anything for me—just saying. But don't get me wrong; if you want go to college and study the sex life of the South American Zoon-A-Boogey frog and live in your mom's basement till you're thirty years old, go for it.

THANK YOU

N OW WE COME to the end of this part of my story. I still have another fifty years' worth of life to tell you about, but this is enough for now. I went to my fifty-year high school reunion last year. I had broken four ribs about two weeks before the reunion, so I was hurting. After all, it was a five-hundred-mile drive to get there. So I was talking to Ted, Don, Larry, and Jim, and they asked how come I was hurting. I told them I had been riding my four-wheeler on the sand dunes and went ass over teakettle and broke four ribs two weeks ago. And here's what they said to me: "It doesn't surprise us none." Well, as I wrap this up, I want to thank you for taking the time to read my story. I am sure that by now you know that I am the best writer in northern Idaho or maybe the whole state of Idaho. In closing, people ask me if I could have done things differently. My answer is yes, I could have done things differently. Would I have? No. I would not have changed my life for anything. How could I change it? I had the best parents and grandparents in the world. This book was written for them. I know that they were looking over my shoulder as I wrote it. They loved me and let me be me. Thanks, Mom and Dad. There are so many other people to thank, but you already know them. They are in the book. Yes, my life has been painful at times, but it was always fun.

Made in the USA
Middletown, DE
27 November 2019